MOVIES
For the Mind

ALSO BY CHARLES DEEMER:

Country Northwestern and other plays
Practical Screenwriting
Patriots
Oregon Fever: An Anthology of Northwest Writing, 1965-1982 (Editor)
Dress Rehearsals: The Education of a Marginal Writer
The Seagull Hyperdrama
Love At Ground Zero
Three Oregon Plays
Emmett's Gift
Midnight Cabaret: The Writings of Ger Moran (Editor)
What Happens Next? An Introduction to Screenwriting
The Deadly Doowop
Selected Stories
Five Screenplays
Seven Plays (finalist, Oregon Book Award)
Elderberry Wine (Editor)
Seven Come Eleven: Stories and Plays, 1969-1999
Screenwright: the Craft of Screenwriting
Ten Sonnets
Christmas at the Juniper Tavern

MOVIES
For the Mind

Volume One

Charles Deemer

The Sextant Press
2006

Copyright © 2006 by Charles Deemer

All rights reserved. No part of this book may be reproduced or transmitted in any form or by any means, electronic or mechanical, including photocopying, recording or by any information storage and retrieval system, except for brief quotations within a review, without permission in writing from the author. Contact Charles Deemer at cdeemer@yahoo.com.

Published by The Sextant Press
Portland, Oregon

http://www.sextantbooks.com

Printed in the United States of America

ISBN 0-9786357-1-X

Cover photograph by Robert Kyllo

CONTENTS

The Brazen Wing: 7

> When Emil learns he has terminal cancer, he takes his grandson Billy on a trip to Idaho to find the old man's first love. Tracking her to a rest home, they take her with them on a camping and fishing adventure. By the time the authorities find them, Emil has decided on his final exit and Billy has learned valuable lessons about life, death and love.

Casanova Does California: 125

> An irate father gives the historic Casanova a magic potion that propels him to present day Venice, California, where he is appalled by his historic reputation, shocked by a porno movie being made about him, and falls in love with the psychiatrist who evaluates his sanity.

Love In The Ruins: 277

> Wes and Hayaam, two students, an American and a Muslim, become attracted to one another in the tense climate of post-9/11 America. Family, friends and history itself oppose their growing love. A retelling of the archetypal "Romeo and Juliet" love story for an Age of Terror.

(A note to the reader: screenplays published here are not in the standard format used in Hollywood but in an alternative format designed for easier reading. For those new to screenplays, each scene begins with a "slugline" that identifies the location, INT. for interior or inside scenes and EXT. for exterior or outside scenes.)

THE BRAZEN WING

When Emil learns he has terminal cancer, he takes his grandson Billy on a trip to his small hometown in Idaho to find the old man's first love. Tracking her to a rest home, they take her with them on a camping and fishing adventure. By the time the authorities find them, Emil has decided on his final exit and Billy has learned valuable lessons about life, death and love.

FADE IN:

EXT. CITY - DAY

A SERIES OF SHOTS

City life.

—a clogged freeway at rush hour.

—a mall parking lot, full, cars roaming for a space.

—busy city streets. Buses, taxis.

EXT. MEDICAL CENTER - DAY

A full parking lot.

A public bus pulls up.

INT. CLINIC - EXAM ROOM - DAY

EMIL COLLINS, 70s, buttons his shirt after an exam.
Sitting with him is his DOCTOR. He hands Emil a prescription.

> DOCTOR: I'm giving you stronger pain medication.

Emil takes the slip of paper.

> EMIL: Tell me straight, doc. How long?

DOCTOR: In the best of worlds, three, four months.

EMIL: In the worst?

DOCTOR: I can get you in a hospice, Emil. You'd be more comfortable there.

EMIL: In other words, any time after I leave here. Does it come gradually or do I fall over?

DOCTOR: It's impossible to predict something like this. I'll call you later this week about the hospice.

INT. CLINIC - PHARMACY - DAY

Emil sits waiting for his prescription. Flipping through a magazine.

WANDA, 50s, approaches.

WANDA: Professor Collins?

Emil doesn't seem to recognize her.

WANDA: Wanda McDonald. I took American Literature from you maybe fifteen years ago.

EMIL: *(distant)* How are you?

WANDA: I'm fine. I want to tell you how much you changed my life. I was so scared

> coming back to school after so long. You inspired me to keep at it. You were so inspirational.

Emil looks embarrassed.

> EMIL: Well, I'm going to assume you graduated then.
>
> WANDA: I went on and got my Masters. I teach American Lit at the community college. You're my model of what a teacher should be.
>
> VOICE ON SPEAKER: Emil Collins.

Emil stands up. He still looks embarrassed.

> EMIL: I'm glad it all worked out.

He heads for the counter.

INT. CLINIC - FRONT DESK - DAY

Emil starts toward the exit. He carries a small bag. He passes the front desk.

ROSE, 20s, the secretary, sees him.

> ROSE: No poetry today, Professor Collins?

Emil stops and turns.

> EMIL: I almost forgot. Here's one. "As long as you and I have arms and lips which are

for kissing and to sing with, who cares if some one-eyed son-of-a-bitch invents an instrument to measure Spring with?" E.E. Cummings.

ROSE: Now my day's complete.

Rose smiles as Emil exits.

EXT. CLINIC - DAY

Emil emerges into a sun-bright day. He takes a deep breath.

He closes his eyes. Another deep breath.

INT. TAVERN - DAY

Emil at the bar with WALLY, 60s, a friend.

WALLY: That's terrible news!

EMIL: Sshh, I don't want the whole galaxy to know. It's not as bad as you think. I've lived a good life, and the world's going to hell in a hand basket. I'm ready to go.

WALLY: Don't say that.

EMIL: I just did.

WALLY: What are you going to do?

EMIL: That's what I've been thinking about. Maybe take a trip. I'm not sure.

EXT. NEIGHBORHOOD - STREET - DAY

A bus pulls to the curb. Emil gets off.

EXT. NEIGHBORHOOD - RHODES HOUSE - DAY

Upper-end homes along a shaded street.

BILLY RHODES, teens, is mowing the front lawn.

Emil slowly approaches.

Billy turns off the lawn mower.

> BILLY: Hey, Gramps! How'd it go?
>
> EMIL: I've got the heart of a linebacker.
>
> BILLY: You should've called. I would've picked you up.
>
> EMIL: You would've, would you? How would you manage that?
>
> BILLY: I'd take Mom's car. It's not that far. And on the way back, you'd be in the car, so driving with my learner's permit would be legal.
>
> EMIL: Next time I have to get somewhere, I'll let you know.

INT. RHODES HOUSE - DINING ROOM -

NIGHT

The family around the dinner table: Besides Emil and Billy, Emil's daughter MARTI and her husband, DON, both late 30s, and Billy's older sister, SARA, 19.

>MARTI: What did the doctor have to say, Dad?
>
>EMIL: I have the heart of a marathon runner.
>
>BILLY: And a linebacker.
>
>EMIL: *(winking at him)* That, too.
>
>MARTI: Your blood pressure's good? Nothing out of order?
>
>EMIL: Everything's out of order. It's called old age.
>
>MARTI: I'm allowed to worry about you.
>
>DON: *(to Marti)* Change of subject. Are you telling her or am I?
>
>SARA: Telling me what?
>
>MARTI: We decided to spend a week at the beach. We're putting you in charge. Think you can handle it?

Sara brightens up.

DON: And no parties. You keep an eye on her, Billy.

SARA: Dad, I'm a sophomore in college. Don't treat me like I'm in high school.

DON: As long as you're home for the summer, you play by the house rules.

SARA: Yes, I can handle it. I'll even cook for these comedians.

EMIL: I can't wait.

EXT. RHODES HOUSE - DRIVEWAY - DAY

Seeing Don and Marti off are Sara and Billy. Don in the car behind the wheel, waiting for Marti to get in.

MARTI: Give me a hug.

She hugs Billy, then Sara.

MARTI: No parties. I mean it.

SARA: Mother, please.

MARTI: I'm calling to check on you.

DON: Marti...

MARTI: We'll be home next Monday night. It may be late.

Marti gets in the car. Don backs out the driveway.

And they are gone.

>BILLY: Are you really going to cook?

>SARA: What I'm going to do, kiddo, is make a deal with you.

INT. RHODES HOUSE - SARA'S BEDROOM - DAY

Sara is packing a tote bag. Billy watches.

>SARA: I'll be back Monday.

>BILLY: What time?

>SARA: I don't know. Afternoon.

>BILLY: How are we going to eat? I don't think Gramps knows how to cook.

>SARA: Gramps has money. He'll take you out every night.

>BILLY: Shouldn't I get something for not telling mom?

Sara takes out her wallet. She hands Billy a twenty dollar bill.

>SARA: Don't ask for more because it's all I have.

> BILLY: Are you going to have sex with him?

EXT. RHODES HOUSE - DRIVEWAY - DAY

Sara with her bag, waiting in the driveway.

INT. RHODES HOUSE - DAY

Emil at the front window. Billy joins him.

> EMIL: Where's Sara going?
>
> BILLY: She's taking off with her boyfriend.
>
> EMIL: Your mother know about this?
>
> BILLY: No way.

Emil studies him.

> EMIL: How much did you get?
>
> BILLY: Twenty bucks.
>
> EMIL: You come too cheap, lad.
>
> BILLY: And the keys to Mom's car. Want to go for a ride later?

EXT. RHODES HOUSE - DRIVEWAY - DAY

A car pulls up. Behind the wheel is JASON, 20s.

Sara climbs in and they're off.

INT. RHODES HOUSE - DAY

Billy and Emil watch Sara leave.

> BILLY: They're going to have sex.

> EMIL: Sex? Remind me what that is again.

Billy grins and Emil musses his hair.

EXT. VW CONVERTIBLE - DAY

Billy driving Marti's red VW convertible. Emil riding shotgun.

Billy's a safe driver. Both are grinning, enjoying themselves.

INT. ICE CREAM PARLOR - DAY

They sit at a table over ice cream sundaes.

> EMIL: I need to take a little trip. Since you're such a great chauffeur, how'd you like to come along?

> BILLY: Where to?

> EMIL: Idaho.

> BILLY: Idaho, wow!

> EMIL: Clearwater country.

BILLY: How far is that?

EMIL: Not far at all. A long day's drive.

BILLY: They come back Monday night.

EMIL: We'll be fine. Leave today, get there tomorrow. Spend a few days. I'll show you God's country and we'll do some fishing.

BILLY: Awesome.

EXT. RHODES HOUSE - DRIVEWAY - DAY

Packing the VW for the trip. The top is down.

Both Emil and Billy are traveling light. Each puts a tote bag in the trunk.

Emil climbs in.

EMIL: I'm ready when you are.

Billy jumps behind the wheel.

BILLY: This is so awesome.

EXT. NEIGHBORHOOD - STREET - DAY

The VW cruising.

EMIL: Pull in over there.

EXT. TAVERN - DAY

Billy pulls in front of the tavern.

> EMIL: I won't be a minute.

INT. TAVERN - DAY

Emil enters and finds Wally at the bar.

> WALLY: *(to bartender)* Bring a beer for Emil.
>
> EMIL: Just here to make a delivery.

He hands Wally an envelope. On it is printed: "Emil Collins. To be opened in the event of death."

> WALLY: Damn it, Emil, why you giving me something like this?
>
> EMIL: It's a copy of my will. I named you executor.
>
> WALLY: I'm not a lawyer.
>
> EMIL: You're a friend. That's what counts.
>
> WALLY: You decide what to do?
>
> EMIL: I ever tell you about Emma?
>
> WALLY: Probably. I don't remember. Who's Emma?
>
> EMIL: The one that got away. I'm going to find her and I'm going to ask her to marry

me.

> WALLY: You can't ask a woman to marry somebody on his death bed.

> EMIL: You don't know Emma.

> WALLY: What if she's already married?

> EMIL: I'll ask her to get divorced.

> WALLY: What if she's dead?

> EMIL: Then I really blew it.

EXT. TAVERN - DAY

Emil comes out and gets back in the car.

> EMIL: To Idaho, James!

Billy grins and starts the engine.

A SERIES OF SHOTS - THE DRIVE TO IDAHO

–on a crowded freeway in the city.

–on an Interstate in the suburbs.

–on an Interstate in countryside.

–at a rest stop, Emil pointing out their destination on a large wall map.

—back on the Interstate, different countryside.

—at a fast food speaker, ordering.

—on the Interstate with burgers in hand.

EXT. INTERSTATE - DAY

The VW top is up. Emil driving.

He takes an exit ramp.

INT. VW CONVERTIBLE - DAY

Billy, who was dozing at the window, stirs.

> BILLY: We need gas?
>
> EMIL: We're calling it a day.
>
> BILLY: Already?
>
> EMIL: We've come about as far as my back can take.

EXT. MOTEL - OFFICE - DAY

The VW parked in front. Billy waits.

Emil comes out, holding up a key.

INT. MOTEL - ROOM - DAY

They each carry a bag into the motel room. Twin double beds.

EMIL: Which bed you want?

Billy tosses his bag onto a bed.

EXT. RESTAURANT - NIGHT

The VW parked in the lot.

INT. RESTAURANT - BOOTH - NIGHT

Emil and Billy finishing up dinner.

>BILLY: Why do you call Idaho God's country?
>
>EMIL: Because it is. Only northern Idaho, to be precise.
>
>BILLY: If it's so great, why'd you leave?
>
>EMIL: Because many, many years ago I decided I should go to college and become a professor. Sometimes life deals you very difficult choices. You do the best you can at the time.
>
>BILLY: How come we never went to Idaho on vacation?
>
>EMIL: Because your mother wouldn't be able to find a five-star resort.

INT. RESTAURANT - BOOTH – NIGHT (LATER)

Billy working on an ice cream sundae. Emil with coffee.

> EMIL: You have a girlfriend?
>
> BILLY: Not really.
>
> EMIL: That almost sounds like yes.
>
> BILLY: She already has a boyfriend.
>
> EMIL: Maybe she really likes you better.
>
> BILLY: Yeah, right.
>
> EMIL: It's not possible?
>
> BILLY: She's a cheerleader. Her boyfriend's a football player.
>
> EMIL: Ah. So you've given up.
>
> BILLY: Wouldn't you?
>
> EMIL: Sometimes we give up too easily.

INT. MOTEL - ROOM - NIGHT

Emil in one bed, Billy in the other. Watching TV.

Emil turns out his bedside lamp.

> EMIL: Goodnight.

BILLY: Want me to turn off TV?

EMIL: Won't bother me at all.

INT. MOTEL - ROOM – NIGHT (LATER)

A dark room. Emil snoring to beat the band.

Billy rolls over. He grabs the second pillow on his bed and holds it over his head.

INT. MOTEL - ROOM - DAY

Emil comes out from the bathroom. Billy is still in bed.

Emil shakes Billy.

EMIL: Rise and shine! One hundred miles before breakfast.

EXT. INTERSTATE - DAY

Emil driving.

INT. VW CONVERTIBLE - DAY

The top up. Billy sprawled on the back seat, sleeping.

EXT. TRUCK STOP - DAY

The VW parked and dwarfed by 18-wheelers.

INT. TRUCK STOP - TABLE - DAY

Billy with eggs, bacon, hot cakes. Emil with oatmeal and coffee.

>EMIL: I have a confession to make.

Billy looks up but says nothing.

>EMIL: I'm looking for someone.

>BILLY: Who?

>EMIL: A woman. The one who got away.

>BILLY: Who's that?

>EMIL: Her name is Emma. I don't even know if she's still alive.

>BILLY: When's the last time you heard from her?

>EMIL: Let me think ... I haven't seen her since 1947. But I talked to her on the phone after that. Once.

>BILLY: You haven't heard from her in all that time?

>EMIL: Don't rub it in.

>BILLY: So why do you want to see her all of a sudden?

Emil stands up.

> EMIL: Desire is one of the wonderful mysteries of life, lad. Excuse me. Nature calls.

He hobbles away. Billy watches him go, puzzled.

EXT. INTERSTATE - INTERCHANGE - DAY

The VW moves off the Interstate onto a state highway.

EXT. HIGHWAY - FARMLAND - DAY

The VW on a two-lane highway through Palouse country.

In the distance, a lone tractor working the land.

INT. VW CONVERTIBLE - DAY

Emil driving. Billy staring off at the tractor.

> BILLY: He has to plow that whole gigantic field?
>
> EMIL: It's called farming.

EXT. HOMESTEAD - OUTSKIRTS - DAY

The VW on the outskirts of a small Idaho town we'll call Homestead.

A junk yard. A gas station or two. A welcoming sign.

EXT. HOMESTEAD - MAIN STREET - DAY

Homestead's Main Street is typically lined with the square, brick and stone buildings of a western town.

Emil pulls the VW in front of a bar.

INT. VW CONVERTIBLE - DAY

Emil keeps the engine running.

> EMIL: Can you amuse yourself for about half an hour?
>
> BILLY: Is she in the bar?
>
> EMIL: I doubt it. I'm just hoping I find somebody I know.
>
> BILLY: Is this a wild goose chase?
>
> EMIL: It's not over till it's over. Be back here in thirty.

INT. BAR - DAY

Emil enters the bar.

Half-a-dozen men sit on stools. A few couples at small tables along a wall.

Most of the men look old enough to be retired, wearing cowboy hats or baseball caps. Emil joins them at the bar.

The BARTENDER, a middle-aged woman, comes over.

> BARTENDER: What can I get you?
>
> EMIL: Short beer. Whatever's on tap.

She goes to draw it.

Emil looks down the bar for a friendly face. Just men lost in their thoughts.

The bartender brings his beer.

> EMIL: I'm looking for Emma Wells. That was her last name when she was single. You wouldn't know her, would you?
>
> BARTENDER: Jake, you know Emma Wells?

An old man down the bar, JAKE, looks up. He just nods.

> BARTENDER: This here fella's looking for her.
>
> EMIL: *(to Jake)* Can I buy you a beer?

EXT. HOMESTEAD - MAIN STREET - DAY

The VW cruising Main Street.

Billy reaches one end of town, turns around, and comes back. The downtown section of Homestead is about three blocks long.

Finally he pulls into a fast food restaurant at one end of town.

INT. FAST FOOD JOINT - DAY

Billy goes to the counter.

INT. BAR - TABLE - DAY

Emil and Jake at a table.

> JAKE: You know Emma's daughter?
>
> EMIL: I didn't know she had a daughter.
>
> JAKE: And two sons. She could give you the address of the place.

INT. FAST FOOD JOINT - DAY

Billy finishing up a burger.

JENNY, teens, comes by, bussing tables. She wears the company uniform.

> JENNY: Everything okay?
>
> BILLY: It's great.
>
> JENNY: You're not from around here.

BILLY: I guess it shows.

JENNY: This is a small town. If you don't know somebody coming in, it usually means they're just passing through.

BILLY: I'm visiting with my granddad. He grew up here.

JENNY: What's his name?

BILLY: Emil Collins.

JENNY: I'll ask my grandma if she knows him. You staying long?

BILLY: Just a few days. He's taking me fishing.

JENNY: Then we have something in common. I'm on the river every chance I get.

BILLY: Actually I've never been fishing before.

EXT. BAR - DAY

Emil comes out. No Billy.

EXT. FAST FOOD JOINT - PARKING LOT - DAY

Jenny has walked Billy to his car. She hands him a slip of paper.

JENNY: Call me. Maybe grandma knows your granddad.

BILLY: Way cool. Thanks.

They exchange smiles. An attraction is obvious.

EXT. BAR - DAY

The VW pulls up.

Emil comes around to the driver's side.

EMIL: Slide over.

Billy does. Emil gets behind the wheel.

EXT. HOMESTEAD - NEIGHBORHOOD - DAY

The VW cruising through a cluster of homes, a small town neighborhood.

Emil pulls to the curb.

EXT. HOME - PORCH - DAY

Emil and Bill at the door, waiting.

MARTHA, 40s, opens the door.

MARTHA: May I help you?

INT. HOME - LIVING ROOM - DAY

Emil and Billy sit on a sofa across the room from Martha.

> MARTHA: I'm trying to raise three kids by myself. I can't look after her, too. Dennis offered his guest room but he lives in LA, and you couldn't get mom there if you paid her.
>
> EMIL: Can't say I blame her.
>
> MARTHA: When we decided it wasn't safe for her to live alone, we had little choice. It's a good facility. Very good reputation.
>
> EMIL: Do you have the address? I'd like to visit her.
>
> MARTHA: Let me get it.

Martha leaves the room.

> EMIL: She looks a little like Emma. Only Emma was prettier.

EXT. HOUSE - PORCH - DAY

Martha seeing them out.

> MARTHA: She doesn't get many visitors, I'm afraid. I can only get up there a weekend every month or so. I'm sure she'll be delighted to see you.
>
> EMIL: I'll give her your best.

INT. HOMESTEAD - STREET - DAY

Emil driving.

> EMIL: It's about an hour. We could get a room and you could stay here if you wanted.
>
> BILLY: You don't mind?
>
> EMIL: Can't be much fun listening to a couple of dinosaurs reminisce.
>
> BILLY: I met a girl who says her grandmother may know you.
>
> EMIL: You met a girl already! Before you were telling me you're the shy type.
>
> BILLY: She wants me to call her later.
>
> EMIL: We'd better get a room.

EXT. HOMESTEAD - MOTEL - DAY

The VW parked in front of a motel door. Emil at the car.

> EMIL: If I'm not back by six, eat without me. You need money?
>
> BILLY: I still have ten bucks.

Emil reaches into his wallet.

Billy's eyes light up when he sees how much Emil is giving him.

> BILLY: Man, thanks!
>
> EMIL: You probably should take that girl out to dinner. I'll fend for myself and catch up with you later.

He gets into the VW.

EXT. COUNTRY ROAD - DAY

The VW, its top down, cruises through farmland down a two-lane highway.

INT. VW CONVERTIBLE - DAY

Emil lost in his thoughts.

INT. GYMNASIUM – NIGHT (FLASHBACK)

SUPER: "Homestead High School Gymnasium. Graduation Prom, 1947."

A crowded dance floor. A SMALL COMBO plays on a temporary stage.

Dancing close are YOUNG EMIL and YOUNG EMMA, teens, in their prom best.

The song ends. Applause.

Emil and Emma move off the dance floor. They pass MR. FRYER.

> MR. FRYER: Emil, I heard Gonzaga gave you a scholarship. Congratulations.
>
> YOUNG EMIL: Thank you, sir.
>
> MR. FRYER: You look beautiful tonight, Emma.
>
> YOUNG EMMA: Thank you, Mr. Fryer.

They move on.

INT. GYMNASIUM - STORAGE ROOM – NIGHT (FLASHBACK)

Emil and Emma sneak into a dark storage room. Lights from the hallway spill through the cracked door.

They immediately embrace and kiss. Hot and heavy.

EXT. UNIVERSITY TOWN - DAY

The VW enters the outskirts of a university town.

INT. HOMESTEAD - MOTEL ROOM - DAY

Billy waiting on the phone.

> BILLY: Jenny?...It's Billy Rhodes. You sold me a hamburger this afternoon....I was wondering if your grandmother knows my granddad....I can't wait to tell him.

He closes his eyes, makes a face, and goes for it.

> BILLY: Say, I was wondering, are you doing anything later?

EXT. UNIVERSITY TOWN - ASSISTED LIVING FACILITY - DAY

The VW pulls into the parking lot.

INT. ASSISTED LIVING FACILITY - COUNTER - DAY

Emil steps up.

> NURSE: May I help you?
>
> EMIL: I'm looking for Emma ...

He glances at the slip of paper Martha gave him.

> EMIL: ...Simpson.

INT. ASSISTED LIVING FACILITY - HALLWAY - DAY

Emil follows the nurse.

> NURSE: Are you a relative?
>
> EMIL: An old friend.
>
> NURSE: I'm sure she'll be happy to see you.

INT. ASSISTED LIVING FACILITY - EMMA'S ROOM - DAY

EMMA, 70s, sits in a stuffed chair. She's staring at a TV soap opera. She looks asleep with her eyes open. A knock on the door.

> NURSE (O.S.): Emma, you have company!

The door opens and the nurse peeks in.

> NURSE: Someone to see you, dear.

Emma turns to the door. Her static expression hasn't changed. Emil appears. He sees Emma – and looks stricken.

EXT. HOMESTEAD - COUNTRY ROAD – NIGHT (FLASHBACK)

A car parked on the shoulder of a deserted road.

INT. CAR – NIGHT (FLASHBACK)

Emil and Emma, prom clothes disheveled and askew, making out. Hotter and heavier.

Emil groans and pulls away.

> YOUNG EMMA: No, I want to. Emil, I want to.

Emil studies her. She kisses him.

> YOUNG EMMA: I want to.

EXT. COUNTRY ROAD – NIGHT (FLASHBACK)

The car door opens. They get out and climb into the back seat.

INT. ASSISTED LIVING FACILITY - EMMA'S ROOM - DAY

The nurse lets Emil in.

> NURSE: I'll let you two visit. Emma, you have company!

Emma just sits there.

> NURSE: It takes her a while, but she'll be with you in a minute.

The nurse leaves, closing the door behind her.

Emil stands inside the doorway.

> EMIL: Emma? It's Emil. Emil Collins.

INT. CAR – NIGHT (FLASHBACK)

Emil on top of Emma. She makes a cry of pain.

> YOUNG EMIL: Emma?

> YOUNG EMMA: It's okay. Don't stop...please, don't stop.

INT. ASSISTED LIVING FACILITY - EMMA'S ROOM - DAY

Emil sits down next to Emma.

> EMIL: Hello, Emma.

Emma's expression finally changes. She looks inquisitive.

> EMMA: Who are you?
>
> EMIL: Emil Collins.
>
> EMMA: Emil...
>
> EMIL: It's been a long time.
>
> EMMA: ...Emil.

Emil takes her hand.

> EMIL: Do you remember me?

She studies him.

> EMMA: Of course, I remember you.

INT. CAR – NIGHT (FLASHBACK)

Young Emil and Emma are in the front seat, dressed, after lovemaking. Her head is on his shoulder.

> YOUNG EMIL: One day I'm going to show you the most incredible sight in God's

creation.

YOUNG EMMA: The Goose Necks.

YOUNG EMIL: You have to see it to believe it. It makes you feel so small – and yet so ... I don't know what the word is. Blessed. To live amidst such wonder. To live amidst such beauty on Earth.

INT. ASSISTED LIVING FACILITY - EMMA'S ROOM - DAY

Emma looks at their joined hands.

EMIL: It's been a long time.

EMMA: I thought you were dead.

EMIL: I should have come long before now. There's so much to talk about. I don't know where to begin. I saw a garden outside. Would you like to go out?

EMMA: Yes, I think I would.

INT. HOMESTEAD - CAFE - DAY (FLASHBACK)

Emil and Emma in a back booth. They lean close and speak in hushed tones.

Emma has been crying.

YOUNG EMIL: It's going to be okay. I just

have to think a minute.

YOUNG EMMA: I'm so scared.

YOUNG EMIL: I'll get a job.

YOUNG EMMA: You can't. You have a scholarship.

YOUNG EMIL: We'll get married. We'll figure a way for me to go to college later.

YOUNG EMMA: I feel so horrible. I feel like I'm ruining your life.

YOUNG EMIL: Emma, stop it. We're in this together.

He takes her hand.

YOUNG EMIL: I love you, Emma.

EXT. ASSISTED LIVING FACILITY - GARDEN - DAY

Emil and Emma walk in the garden.

EMMA: It's so lovely.

EMIL: I was worried when I saw you. You looked so ...

EMMA: Dead? It's boredom. I am so bored in this place!

They walk a moment.

> EMIL: I came here for a reason, Emma. I didn't know if I'd find you or not. But if I did, I had something I had to tell you. I'm going to say it now and get it off my chest. You don't have to say anything. Just listen.
>
> EMMA: Well, you certainly have my attention.
>
> EMIL: I've always regretted not marrying you when I had the chance.
>
> EMMA: What a sweet thing to say.
>
> EMIL: It broke my heart when you married somebody else.

Emma turns away.

EXT. HOMESTEAD - WELLS HOME - DAY (FLASHBACK)

Emil waiting on the front porch. Emma opens the door.

> YOUNG EMMA: Emil, what are you doing here?
>
> YOUNG EMIL: I need to speak to your father.
>
> YOUNG EMMA: Why?

> YOUNG EMIL: I'm going to ask his permission to marry you.
>
> YOUNG EMMA: You can't tell him!
>
> YOUNG EMIL: I'm just asking for your hand. May I see him?
>
> YOUNG EMMA: *(frantic)* No, I think we should wait.
>
> YOUNG EMIL: There's no point.
>
> YOUNG EMMA: But I was just about to call you. I have news. Everything's changed, Emil. It was what they call a false pregnancy. You can go to Gonzaga, after all. We can write and see each other during the holidays, just like we planned.

Emil looks stunned. Emma embraces him.

> YOUNG EMMA: It can be just like it was before.

But there are tears in her eyes.

EXT. HOMESTEAD - MOTEL - DAY

Billy waits outside the hotel room.

A car pulls up. Jenny is driving.

Billy gets in.

INT. JENNY'S CAR - DAY

Jenny wears casual clothes. She's all smiles.

> JENNY: I'm glad you called.

> BILLY: Me, too.

EXT. HOMESTEAD - MOTEL - DAY

Jenny's car pulls away and onto Main Street.

INT. ASSISTED LIVING FACILITY - DINING ROOM - DAY

Emil and Emma seated at a table. RUTH, who works in the kitchen, sets a piece of pie in front of each of them.

> RUTH: Here we go. Mr. Collins, if this isn't the best coconut pie you've ever tasted, you let me know.

> EMIL: It looks delicious.

> RUTH: Only the best for my girl.

She beams at Emma. Emma smiles back. Then Ruth goes back to the kitchen.

An awkward silence.

> EMIL: Do they let you off the premises?

EMMA: It isn't a prison, if that's what you mean. But they're responsible for me. I have to sign out.

EMIL: I was wondering if you'd like to go fishing with me.

EMMA: I remember how much you like to fish.

EMIL: I haven't done much lately. City life, you know. I live with my daughter.

EMMA: Tell me about your family.

EMIL: After you answer my question. Do you want to go fishing?

EMMA: I'm not sure they'd let me go without supervision. They'd be afraid I'd slip on a rock and drown myself.

EMIL: I'd be there.

EMMA: They'd be worried about you for the same reason.

EMIL: How about you sneak out?

EMMA: Oh my!

EMIL: I'm serious. I come by early in the morning, before anybody's up, and take you fishing.

EMMA: That sounds like a real adventure.

EMIL: You always were the adventurous kind. We'd spend the day fishing and then I'd bring you back.

EXT. RIVER - DAY

Jenny's car is parked on the shoulder. Below, the river.

On the bank, Jenny is preparing her pole. Billy stands beside her, holding another pole, looking like he has no idea what to do with it.

JENNY: You never even cast before?

BILLY: You don't get a lot of chances to fish in the city.

JENNY: So we'll start at the beginning. First, you bait your hook.

EXT. ASSISTED LIVING FACILITY - PARKING LOT - DAY

Emil and Emma stand at the VW.

EMIL: I'm going to be here at five in the morning. Don't you change your mind on me.

EMMA: I'll be here.

EMIL: Good. We'll have ourselves quite a

day.

He moves forward. They awkwardly embrace.

EXT. RIVER - DAY

Jenny stands behind Billy, showing him how to cast.

He casts, reels it in, and casts again.

He's a quick learner.

EXT. COUNTRY ROAD - DAY

Emil in the VW, heading back to Homestead.

EXT. RIVER - DAY

Billy with his line in the water. Beside him, Jenny has her line in the water.

Billy is finally fishing on his own.

Above, on the road, the VW passes Jenny's car and heads on.

EXT. HOMESTEAD - SPORTING GOODS STORE - DAY

The VW parked outside a sporting goods store.

INT. SPORTING GOODS STORE - DAY

Emil pushing a cart through the store.

A tent, a camp stove, three sleeping bags, other camping equipment piled in the cart.

EXT. RIVER - DAY

Billy has a fish on the line. He reels it in, and Jenny nets it.

> BILLY: Is it a salmon?
>
> JENNY: A trout. You did great!

She raises a hand. Billy high-fives.

EXT. HOMESTEAD - MOTEL - DAY

Jenny's car pulls behind the VW and stops. They both get out.

Billy sees all the camping gear in the VW.

> JENNY: Are you going camping?
>
> BILLY: I thought we were going fishing.
>
> JENNY: They go together.

INT. MOTEL - ROOM - DAY

Emil is dozing on a bed when the door opens. Billy and Jenny step in.

Emil twitches awake.

JENNY: I'd better go.

BILLY: We'll be there.

JENNY: If you can't, give me a call.

She flashes her smile.

JENNY: I had a great time, Billy.

BILLY: Me, too.

She's gone.

Emil sits up.

EMIL: Who had a great time?

BILLY: Jenny. Her grandmother remembers you.

EXT. HOMESTEAD - RESIDENTIAL STREET - NIGHT

The VW is parked in a driveway.

INT. HOUSE - DINING ROOM - NIGHT

Around the table are Emil, Billy, and Jenny's grandmother, ANNIE, 60s. The table is filled with serving plates of food.

EMIL: I'll take your word for it.

ANNIE: You helped me with my homework

several times. Especially Shakespeare. I hated reading that stuff.

BILLY: You don't remember, Gramps?

EMIL: I remembered to put on my pants this morning. After that, it gets iffy.

Jenny enters with one fried breaded trout on a plate.

JENNY: Ta da! To the fisherman goes the fish!

She places the fish in front of him.

BILLY: Wow.

EMIL: Looks to me like you had a good teacher.

He winks at Jenny. She grins.

ANNIE: I don't know about the rest of you, but I'm starving. Everybody dig in.

They do.

INT. HOUSE - DEN - NIGHT

Billy and Jenny are playing a video game.

INT. HOUSE - KITCHEN - NIGHT

Emil is drying dishes. Annie washes.

> ANNIE: I hardly knew Emma at all. My older sister, bless her soul, got close to her when Emma was pregnant. It was such a bad time for her.
>
> EMIL: She had a difficult pregnancy?
>
> ANNIE: Not being married and all. Everybody knew. I don't know what she would've done if Brad hadn't done the honorable thing and married her. Then, no sooner does she have the baby, and God takes her back. Emma's had such a tragic life.

Emil looks intense. All this is news to him.

EXT. HOUSE - PORCH - NIGHT

Everyone on the porch.

> ANNIE: Hope to see you again before you leave.
>
> EMIL: It was a wonderful dinner. Thanks so much.
>
> JENNY: Call me, Billy?

Billy nods.

INT. VW CONVERTIBLE - NIGHT

Emil driving.

> EMIL: I like her. Maybe she can visit us at the campground.
>
> BILLY: That would be cool.

INT. MOTEL - NIGHT

Both in bed, getting ready for lights out.

> EMIL: I'll shake you at four.
>
> BILLY: You're kidding.
>
> EMIL: I'm serious, lad. We pick Emma up at five.
>
> BILLY: Why so early?
>
> EMIL: We have to get her out of there before the full staff comes on. She's not supposed to go.
>
> BILLY: Like we're helping her escape?
>
> EMIL: Exactly like that. So lights out. Four will be here before you know it.

EXT. MOTEL - DAY

Early morning. Emil and Billy come out. Billy walks like he's half-asleep.

EXT. COUNTRY ROAD - DAY

Emil driving.

Ahead, the horizon getting light.

EXT. ASSISTED LIVING FACILITY - DAY

The VW pulls up and stops.

INT. VW CONVERTIBLE - DAY

Emil lets the engine idle.

Billy is asleep against the window.

EXT. ASSISTED LIVING FACILITY - DAY

Emil gets out.

He looks around. What now?

A sound.

> EMMA: Emil...

Emma steps out of the shadows. She's carrying a small bag.

> EMIL: Let me help you.

He takes her bag. They walk to the car.

Emil taps on the window. Billy jumps awake.

> EMIL: My grandson.

Billy opens the door.

> EMIL: Billy, this is Emma. Would you mind riding in the back seat?

Billy yawns.

> BILLY: Hi. No problem.

> EMMA: Look at all this. How long are we staying?

> EMIL: Hey, if we have a good time, maybe we'll never come back.

He helps Emma in. He moves around the car and gets back behind the wheel.

INT. VW CONVERTIBLE - DAY

Emil smiles.

> EMIL: When it warms up, we'll put the top down.

A SERIES OF SHOTS

as they drive to the campground.

–back along the country road, the sun low and climbing.

–through Homestead as the town wakes up.

–along the river.

INT. ASSISTED LIVING AREA - HALLWAY - DAY

The nurse from earlier comes down the hall. She taps on Emma's door.

Nothing.

Louder.

She unlocks the door.

INT. EMMA'S ROOM - DAY

The nurse looks inside. Nobody home.

INT. ASSISTED LIVING AREA - KITCHEN - DAY

Nurse enters. Ruth at the stove.

> NURSE: Have you seen Emma this morning?
>
> RUTH: Sure haven't.

INT. MARTHA'S HOME - DAY

Martha on the phone.

> MARTHA: God, she must have dementia. Why else would she just wander off?...Don't you think you should call the police?

EXT. CAMPGROUND - DAY

The VW enters a campground.

A few campers here and there.

Emil pull into a campsite right on the river.

Everybody piles out.

> EMMA: It's beautiful!
>
> BILLY: I caught a trout in this river.
>
> EMIL: And ate it, too.

A SERIES OF SHOTS

as they set up camp.

–unloading the car.

–putting up the tent.

–setting up the stove.

–inflating air mattresses for the sleeping bags.

–and then to the river, fishing.

EXT. CAMPGROUND - RIVER - DAY

Everyone fishing from the bank.

Billy and Emma hook a fish almost at the same

time. Great excitement.

Emil helps, netting each trout in turn.

LATER

Emil and Billy on the river alone.

Emma reading at the picnic table.

Emil moves close to where Billy is fishing.

> EMIL: Where would you be if you were a fish? In faster water or slower?
>
> BILLY: I don't know.
>
> EMIL: Think about it. Try and think like a fish.

Billy thinks a moment.

> BILLY: Slower.
>
> EMIL: Why?
>
> BILLY: I'd spend less energy fighting the current.
>
> EMIL: *(grinning)* Good genes, lad. You're a natural. Now see that submerged rock?

Billy follows Emil's gesture.

> EMIL: I bet there's a whale just waiting for

dinner on the upstream side. If you cast right, you can fool him into thinking you're it. Cast right above, so it floats by. Yum yum.

Billy reels in. He recasts near the rock. Almost immediately he gets a strike.

> BILLY: Wow!
>
> EMIL: It's all about observation and thinking like a fish.

INT. RHODES HOME - DAY

A telephone in the living room rings. And rings.

Finally the voice mail picks up.

> MARTI'S VOICE: You've reached the Rhodes residence, Marti, Don, Sara and Billy. Leave a message and the appropriate party will get back to you.

A beep.

INT. COASTAL RESORT - DECK - DAY

Marti with a cell phone on the deck of a five-star resort. Beyond, the spectacular ocean.

> MARTI: Sara, it's mom. Just checking in. Give me a call on my cell when you get a chance. We're blessed with just beautiful weather here. Hope all is well on the home

front. Call me. Love you.

EXT. CAMPGROUND - NIGHT

Evening, just after sunset.

Emma at the stove. Frying trout.

Billy at the campfire, staring into the flames.

INT. TENT - NIGHT

Emil pops a pain pill, chasing it with a can of pop.

Deep breaths.

EXT. CAMPGROUND - NIGHT

Emil comes out of the tent.

> EMIL: Man, that smells good!
>
> EMMA: Almost ready.

EXT. CAMPGROUND - CAMPFIRE - NIGHT

A lantern on the picnic table.

All three around the campfire.

Emil and Emma huddled close.

> BILLY: I'm going for a walk.
>
> EMIL: Take the flashlight.

Billy leaves.

> EMIL: How long were you and Brad married?
>
> EMMA: 40 years. He died not long after our ruby anniversary. And how long were you married? You haven't said much about your wife.
>
> EMIL: Which one?
>
> EMMA: How many were there?
>
> EMIL: Three.
>
> EMMA: Three!
>
> EMIL: Four if you count a live-in girlfriend.
>
> EMMA: Emil Collins. I had no idea you were such a ... what is the word?
>
> EMIL: Idiot?
>
> EMMA: Any children?
>
> EMIL: I live with my daughter. I don't think I'd like her if we weren't related.

EXT. CAMPGROUND - ANOTHER AREA - NIGHT

Billy at a pay phone outside the restrooms.

INT. HOME - BEDROOM - NIGHT

Jenny sprawled on her bed.

INTERCUT

>JENNY: I know that campground very well.

>BILLY: Think you can come?

>JENNY: I can visit. I don't know if I can stay over.

>BILLY: Either way would be great.

EXT. CAMPGROUND - CAMPFIRE - NIGHT

Emil has his arm around Emma. Less romantic, more protection against the chill. Both staring into the fire.

>EMIL: I didn't realize you'd lost a child.

Emma looks up and pulls away.

>EMMA: Who told you that?

>EMIL: Jenny's grandmother, Annie, said her older sister knew you. I'm sorry you had to go through that.

>EMMA: What else did she say?

>EMIL: That seemed like enough.

A silence.

Emma gets up and goes to the stove on the table.

> EMMA: Coffee?
>
> EMIL: I'm fine.
>
> EMMA: I want to take a drive tomorrow. It's not far from here.
>
> EMIL: What isn't?
>
> EMMA: What I want to show you.

Billy returns.

> BILLY: I'm going to bed.
>
> EMMA: Half a cup of coffee and I'm right behind you.
>
> BILLY: Are we all sleeping in the tent?
>
> EMIL: There's room. You need privacy?
>
> BILLY: Not really.

INT. TENT - NIGHT

Emil holds the lantern.

Three sleeping bags in a row on air mattresses.

> EMIL: Take the end there, Billy. I'm beside you.
>
> EMMA: Goodnight, all.

She and Billy crawl into the end sleeping bags.

> EMIL: I'll try not to step on you, lad.

He turns off the lantern.

He maneuvers over Billy and crawls into the middle sleeping bag.

Emma laughs.

> EMIL: What's so funny?
>
> EMMA: I'm so bored most of the time, the nurses have me on my death bed. If only they could see me now.

INT. COASTAL RESORT - DAY

Marti on the phone.

Don enters from the bathroom.

> MARTI: Nobody's answering. Since when has either of them been out of the house at eight without me kicking them in the butt?
>
> DON: Your dad's not answering?
>
> MARTI: No one is home.

She slams down the receiver.

> DON: No.
>
> MARTI: What?
>
> DON: We're not rushing back. We're not letting this ruin our vacation.
>
> MARTI: Oh my God. What if Dad's in the hospital? That would explain why no one is home.

She punches a number.

> MARTI: How do I get information?

EXT. CAMPGROUND - RIVER - DAY

Early morning. Emil alone at the river.

He folds his arms against the chill. Contemplative.

EXT. CAMPGROUND - DAY

Emil has coffee on. Emma stumbles out of the tent, looking a fright.

> EMMA: Good morning.
>
> EMIL: Yes, it is.
>
> EMMA: I slept like a rock.

EXT. CAMPGROUND - DAY LATER)

Emil and Emma at the table, eating breakfast.

Billy steps out of the tent.

>EMIL: Morning. I kept your eggs warm.

INT. FAST FOOD JOINT - DAY

Jenny behind the counter.

Two deputies enter. They are DEP. HALL and DEP. MALINOWSKI.

>JENNY: Morning. What will it be?

>DEP. HALL: Just coffee.

>DEP. MALINOWSKI: Decaf, black.

>DEP. HALL: Real coffee, room for cream.

He hands Jenny a flier.

>DEP. HALL: You seen this woman?

THE FLIER

a photo of Emma with description and the words, "Missing from the Palouse Valley Assisted Living Center."

>JENNY: I don't know her. Would you like me to put this on our bulletin board?

DEP. HALL: You took the words right out of my mouth.

EXT. CAMPGROUND - DAY

Emil and Emma in the VW with the top down.

> EMIL: We should be back before dinner.
>
> BILLY: Maybe I'll have a trout dinner waiting for you. Jenny's coming by. She can help.
>
> EMIL: *(to Emma)* Romeo here used to be shy with girls.

Emil toots the horn – and they're off.

INT. FAST FOOD JOINT - DAY

Jenny on the phone.

> JENNY: I don't get off till three, so it'll be four or so. Is that too late?...Okay, great! See you then.

She hangs up.

YVONNE, a teen co-worker, has overheard.

> YVONNE: New boyfriend?
>
> JENNY: I'm not sure yet.

EXT. COUNTRY ROAD - DAY

The VW, top down, Emil at the wheel, Emma's hair blowing in the wind.

EXT. COUNTRY CEMETERY - ROAD - DAY

The VW pulls into a small cemetery.

> EMMA: Park anywhere.

EXT. COUNTRY CEMETERY - GRAVES - DAY

Emma leads the way past rows of graves.

She stops at a small marker.

Emil reads: "Emily Sharon Simpson. 1948-1950."

> EMIL: Your daughter?

> EMMA: Our daughter.

Emil looks confused.

> EMIL: I'm missing something.

> EMMA: I'd decided to get an abortion. I didn't want you to turn down your scholarship.

> EMIL: Emma...if you'd told me—

> EMMA: I couldn't go through with it. I

> named her Emily, after you. She was so beautiful.
>
> EMIL: But what about Brad?
>
> EMMA: He always had a thing for me. He talked me into keeping the baby and marrying him. Everyone thought it was his.
>
> EMIL: But did you love him?
>
> EMMA: Yes, I did come to love him. Mostly I've had a happy life. Isn't that crazy?

Emma loses herself in Emil's arms.

EXT. CAMPGROUND - DAY

Jenny pulls up and parks. She gets out.

She walks down to the river where Billy is fishing. A smile on her face.

EXT. RIVER - DAY

Jenny sneaks up behind Billy. She grabs him.

He turns, and they playfully wrestle a moment.

> JENNY: Catch anything?
>
> BILLY: Take a look.

She peeks in an ice chest on the bank. Three trout.

JENNY: I think you're getting the hang of this.

EXT. COUNTRY CEMETERY - DAY

Emil and Emma strolling, holding hands.

EMIL: I told Billy we'd be back by dinner.

EXT. CAMPGROUND - TABLE - DAY

Jenny has the fish breaded and ready to fry.

Billy setting the table.

BILLY: Here they come.

The VW arrives and parks.

Emil and Emma get out.

Seeing Emma, Jenny does a double-take. The lady on the poster.

EMIL: This must be Jenny!

JENNY: Hello.

BILLY: My granddad. And this is Emma.

EMMA: Hi.

Jenny looks ill at ease. Yes, she's definitely the one on the poster.

EXT. CAMPGROUND - CAMPFIRE - NIGHT

Everyone around a campfire.

Billy gets up.

>BILLY: Be right back.

>EMIL: Seeing a man about a horse?

>BILLY: Right.

>JENNY: I'll come with you.

EXT. CAMPGROUND - WALKWAY - NIGHT

Jenny takes Billy's arm.

>JENNY: She's a missing person.

>BILLY: Who is?

>JENNY: Emma. A sheriff came in with a missing poster about her.

EXT. CAMPGROUND - CAMPFIRE - NIGHT

Emil and Emma, sitting close.

Billy and Jenny return.

>EMIL: Everything come out all right?

>BILLY: Can I talk to you a minute, Gramps?

Emil gives a "what is this about?" look to Emma. He gets up.

Billy moves away. Emil follows him into the growing darkness.

EXT. CAMPGROUND - TENT - NIGHT

Billy stops near the tent. Low tones.

> BILLY: There's a wanted poster out for Emma. They think she's been kidnapped or something.

> EMIL: Oh, boy.

INT. COASTAL RESORT - NIGHT

Marti on the phone once again. Don on the bed, reading.

> MARTI: I have no idea what's going on. Sara's not answering her cell. I called every hospital I could think of....Well, if anything changes, you have my number.

She hangs up.

> MARTI: Vicky says there are four papers in the driveway. Starting with the day we left.

> DON: That's doesn't make sense. Emil always reads the paper.

> MARTI: Nobody's home, Don. That's what

> I've been trying to tell you.
>
> DON: Where would they go?
>
> MARTI: I have no idea. But we can't find out sitting here thinking about it.
>
> DON: Marti—
>
> MARTI: If you don't want to come, I'll rent a car in the morning.

EXT. CAMPGROUND - CAMPFIRE - NIGHT

Everyone around the fire. Jenny gets up.

> JENNY: I have to get back. Sorry to be the bearer of bad news.
>
> EMMA: At my age, a little notoriety does the soul good.
>
> JENNY: I just hope no one gets in trouble.
>
> BILLY: I'll walk you to the car.

They disappear into the night.

> EMIL: At least we had our time on the river.

A reflective moment.

> EMIL: *(quoting from memory)* "I do not know what it is about you that closes and opens; only something in me understands

the voice of your eyes is deeper than all roses. Nobody, not even the rain, has such small hands." *(softly)* Cummings.

EMMA: I don't want to go back.

EMIL: We don't have much choice.

EMMA: Of course we do. What is it the brochures say? We're in our golden years. Don't you feel golden?

Emil looks away, thinking.

EMMA: What is it?

EMIL: Staying here sounds so wonderful. But don't you think they'd find us pretty quick?

EMMA: We don't have to stay here. Where is that place you used to tell me about? Your family took a vacation there. How you raved about it! The goose something?

EMIL: The Goose Necks of the San Juan. The most amazing scenery on the planet.

EMMA: Let's go there.

EXT. CAMPGROUND - PARKING AREA - NIGHT

Billy and Jenny in a lip lock. It ends.

JENNY: I guess that means I'll see you soon.

BILLY: You don't think Gramps will get in trouble, will he?

JENNY: It's not like he took her against her will. I think everybody will be thrilled she's okay.

EXT. CAMPGROUND - CAMPFIRE - NIGHT

The sound of Jenny's car leaving.

Billy appears from the shadows.

BILLY: So are we going back first thing in the morning or can I fish first?

EMIL: Change of plans. We're going into town and renting a car. You return to Homestead and Emma and I are going on a trip.

BILLY: But she's a missing person.

EMMA: Do I look lost to you?

BILLY: A trip where?

EMIL: To God's most amazing creation.

EXT. COASTAL RESORT - DAY

Don is packing the car. Marti brings out another suitcase.

There is visible friction between them.

EXT. CAMPGROUND - DAY

Breaking camp. Almost done.

Emil at the car. Emma wiping down the table.

Billy brings the rolled tent to the car.

> BILLY: I want to go.
>
> EMIL: That's not a good idea.
>
> BILLY: Why not?
>
> EMIL: Because your mother would kill me.
>
> BILLY: I'll leave her a message so she knows we're safe. Gramps, it's summer. I've got nothing else to do. You know we'd make better time with me driving. I mean, it can't take that long to get there. They won't even be home yet. They probably won't even know the difference.
>
> EMIL: Your dad would know. He'd see the mileage on the car.
>
> BILLY: Big deal. We bought our own gas, didn't we?

Emma walks up.

> EMIL: He wants to come. What do you think?
>
> EMMA: What I really think? I wish I had the courage at his age to do something this adventurous.

Billy smiles, as if it's settled.

> EMIL: You're not leaving anybody a message.

A SERIES OF SHOTS – INTERCUT

The two journeys

–Emil, Emma and Billy on a country road.

–Marti and Don on the highway from the coast.

–The VW catches a highway to head south.

–The Rhodes car reaches the outskirts of the city.

INT. RHODES HOME - DAY

Marti rushes in. She goes straight to the phone.

She picks it up and punches a number. Voice mail.

> DOCTOR *(FILTERED)*: This is a message for Emil. I found a hospice with a vacancy but I need to hear from you right away so I can reserve it for you. Please get back to me as soon as you can.

Don enters. Marti looks in shock.

> DON: What's the matter?

> MARTI: My father is dying.

EXT. GOLF COURSE - DAY

A twosome, one of whom is the doctor. His PARTNER is teeing up.

The doctor's cell phone rings.

> DOCTOR: Wouldn't you know?

He steps away and answers it.

> DOCTOR: Hello? ... Yes, Mrs. Rhodes. .... What? ... Mrs. Rhodes, your father has pancreatic cancer. He has a few months at best.

INT. RHODES HOUSE - DAY

Marti sets down the phone. Total shock.

EXT. DESERT SOUTHWEST - DAY

The VW convertible zipping along with the top down.

Billy is driving. Luggage has been rearranged, so Emil and Emma can sit together in the back seat.

Their hair blows in the wind. They have the ecstatic look of teenagers in love.

And the landscape, the landscape!

Spectacular rock formations rise from the ground like stone gods marching across the desert. The beauty is enough to turn an atheist religious.

EXT. RHODES HOUSE - DAY

A police car is parked in the driveway.

INT. RHODES HOUSE - LIVING ROOM - DAY

OFFICER HAMILTON filling out Marti's missing person report. She's been crying. Don looks stoic.

> OFFICER HAMILTON: But you have no idea where they might have gone?

Marti shakes her head.

> OFFICER HAMILTON: No brother or sister to visit, old friend, anyone at all who comes to mind?

> DON: He always talked about going back to Homestead before he died.

> OFFICER HAMILTON: Where's the homestead?

> DON: It's a small town in northern Idaho.

EXT. RHODES HOUSE - POLICE CAR - DAY

Officer Hamilton in the car, punching numbers in a computer. Waiting for results.

INT. RHODES HOUSE - DAY

Hamilton walks in through the open door. Marti waits for him.

> OFFICER HAMILTON: Does the name Emma Simpson mean anything to you?
>
> MARTI: Don! Did dad ever mention someone named Emma?

Don approaches.

> DON: You know, it rings a bell. Sometimes he'd talk about his first girlfriend back home. I believe it was an Emma.

EXT. HOMESTEAD - FAST FOOD JOINT - DAY

A Sheriff's car pulls in and parks.

INT. FAST FOOD JOINT - DAY

The deputies Hall and Malinowski come to Jenny at the counter.

> DEP. HALL: Got another poster for you.

He hands it to Jenny.

THE POSTER

shows Emil, Billy, and Sara.

Looking over her shoulder is Yvonne.

YVONNE: Is that his girlfriend?

Jenny looks dazed.

EXT. CAMPGROUND - DAY

Sheriff's car pulls into the old campsite. The two deputies get out.

One kicks a burned log in the makeshift fireplace.

The other stares out at the river.

DEP. HALL: What makes a grown adult a missing person?

DEP. MALINOWSKI: Dementia?

DEP. HALL: Maybe they just wanted to go fishing.

EXT. SOUTHERN UTAH - GOOSE NECKS AREA - DAY

The sun low in the west.

The VW convertible pulls up atop a flat mesa. Nothing but the wide open spaces up here. This is definitely not "an improved camping area."

Billy, driving, gets out. Emil and Emma get out from the back seat.

Emma does a complete circle, sucking in the view. Her hair blows – there's a good wind way up here!

> EMMA: Oh my Lord!

> EMIL: This is just the first course. Follow me.

Emil starts across the mesa. Emma and Billy follow.

EXT. GOOSE NECKS - MESA - DAY

Suddenly the ground opens up into a deep gash. No warning, just a sudden drop.

Emil makes sure everyone stops in time.

Across the canyon, the mesa continues. The perspective is misleading – so far down, that the canyon gives the illusion that one could jump across it.

> EMIL: Be really careful – but look down there.

He takes Emma's hand and leads her closer to the edge. Billy follows.

They get close enough to peer down the deep canyon.

> EMIL: I give you – the Goose Necks of the San Juan River.

EXT. GOOSE NECKS - DAY

And what an incredible view!

Far, far below, the thin river turns one way and then back on itself, for as far as the eye can see.

It's like a condensed version of the Grand Canyon – and more spectacular because it's more comprehensible. You see it and wonder...Could I really jump across?

EXT. GOOSE NECKS - MESA - DAY

Emma is blown away by the beauty. She takes Emil's arms. Tears well in her eyes.

> EMIL: What do you think, Billy?

> BILLY: I think this is what awesome really means.

INT. RHODES HOUSE - NIGHT

Suitcases at the door. Don waiting patiently.

Marti storms up.

EXT. AIRPORT - NIGHT

A small jetliner landing.

INT. AIRPORT - TERMINAL - NIGHT

Marti and Don enter. Don totes a carry-on, Marti has a cell phone to her ear.

She lowers it.

> MARTI: I'm going to murder that girl.

INT. AIRPORT - RENTAL CAR COUNTER - NIGHT

Don at the counter. Marti waits nearby.

EXT. AIRPORT - RENTAL CAR PICKUP - NIGHT

Don and Marti climb into a late model car.

INT. RENTAL CAR - NIGHT

Don behind the wheel.

> MARTI: Do you know where you're going?
>
> DON: I know what the map says. Do you have a short cut?

Marti glares at him, then out the window.

EXT. MESA - SCRUB BRUSH - NIGHT

The tent is set up within a cluster of scrub brush, protected somewhat from the wind.

No table. No fireplace. Primitive camping.

Everyone sits on a tarp on the ground. The stove, also on the ground, is nearby.

Emma looking up at the sky.

> EMMA: A shooting star! Emil, help me up.

He has a bit of trouble getting up himself. Then he offers Emma his hand.

Billy jumps up. They all look up at the sky.

> BILLY: There's one!

> EMMA: And another!

Overhead, a summer meteor shower in its early tease.

The Milky Way floats across the sky like the ghost of a dragon.

> EMMA: I've never been anywhere so beautiful.

EXT. HOMESTEAD - MOTEL - NIGHT

The rental car parked in front of the office.

Marti waiting in the car.

INT. MOTEL - ROOM - NIGHT

Don turns on the light, and they enter.

> MARTI: Did you ask about a restaurant?
>
> DON: Nothing open this late.
>
> MARTI: Terrific. Welcome to Redneck City.
>
> DON: There's a bar that may make us a burger.

INT. HOMESTEAD - BAR - NIGHT

Don enters alone. A decent late night crowd, mostly male and blue collar.

Don walks to the end of the bar.

The LADY BARTENDER comes over.

> DON: Is the kitchen still open?

LATER

Don sitting at the bar, nursing a beer, waiting for the food.

A RANCHER takes the stool next to him.

> RANCHER: *(to bartender)* Regular, Doris!

The rancher looks at Don.

> DON.: I was wondering if you knew Emil Collins or Emma Simpson.

The rancher grins.

> RANCHER: What are you, an uncover cop from Boise? Well, I don't know where the hell they are for one, for two I wouldn't tell you if I did, and for three, whatever the hell they've done, it can't be worse than being cooped up in a damn rest home somewhere.

EXT. BAR - NIGHT

Don comes out, carrying a sack of burgers.

EXT. MESA - NIGHT

Only Emil and Emma outside now. Still looking up at the meteor shower.

> EMMA: *(counting meteors)* Two hundred and five.

> EMIL: One eighty-four. Eighty-five!

> EMMA: Two hundred and six!

INT. HOMESTEAD - MOTEL - NIGHT

Marti and Don at the table. Eating burgers and fries for dinner.

The phone rings.

Marti dashes for it.

INT. RHODES HOUSE - NIGHT

Sara making the call. Her boyfriend, Jason, stands next to her.

> SARA: She's going to kill me.

INTERCUT

> MARTI: Hello.
>
> SARA: *(meekly)* It's me.
>
> MARTI: Where have you been? Where's your brother and granddad?
>
> SARA: I don't know. Is Gramps really dying?
>
> MARTI: No thanks to you. You are grounded forever!

Don comes forward.

> DON: Give me the phone.

Marti clutches it.

> SARA: It was an emergency. Jason needed to go out of town for a job interview and needed moral support. On the way back we had a flat, and then his spare ended up

>   being flat, and—

Don has wrestled away the phone.

>   DON: It's me. Did they mention anything about coming to Idaho?
>
>   SARA: They're in Idaho? *(to Jason)* They're in Idaho.

EXT. MESA - NIGHT

Holding hands, Emil and Emma slowly walk to the tent.

Before going in, Emma stops him. She kisses him.

>   EMMA: You haven't talked about your health.

He looks suspicious.

>   EMIL: Do I look dead or something?
>
>   EMMA: I was wondering if, you know, you're sexually active.
>
>   EMIL: I haven't been for years.
>
>   EMMA: The machinery broke?
>
>   EMIL: Oh, no. Now and again I rise in the morning, if you know what I mean.
>
>   EMMA: You just have nothing to do with it.

Well, now you do.

INT. TENT - NIGHT

Awkward, comic, Emil and Emma try to crawl into one sleeping bag without waking Billy, who sleeps nearby with only the empty bag between them.

> EMIL: *(whispering)* This will never work.
>
> EMMA: *(whispering)* We won't know unless we try.

They maneuver into the bag together, Emil angled above her. Now they struggle to get their pants off.

It's not an easy thing to do – and in the process Emma gets the giggles.

> EMIL: Sshh.

But trying to stop her only gives him the giggles.

> BILLY: What's so funny?

This gets them laughing louder.

> BILLY: Have you two been drinking?

And louder still.

> BILLY: You are really weird.

Emil and Emma manage to get control of themselves.

> EMIL: *(whispering)* He's right.

Which gets them laughing again.

EXT. MESA - CAMPING AREA - DAY

On the tarp, Emma is zipping two sleeping bags together.

Billy comes out of the tent.

> BILLY: Morning.
>
> EMMA: Good morning, Billy.
>
> BILLY: Where's Gramps?
>
> EMMA: He headed off yonder with a shovel. Sorry we woke you up.
>
> BILLY: What was so funny?

Emma starts to reply but laughs instead. She raises a hand, as if excusing herself.

Billy, shaking his head, wanders off.

INT. TENT - DAY

Emma comes in with the zipped-together bag. She makes room for it.

Moving Emil's travel bag, a small bottle of medicine drops out.

Emma picks it up and reads the label.

An immediate expression of concern.

EXT. MESA - DAY

Emil approaching camp without the shovel.

Emma coming out to meet him.

> EMIL: I gave Billy the shovel if you need it.
>
> EMMA: Why are you in pain? I found your pills. What's going on, Emil? I want the truth.

EXT. MESA - CAMPFIRE - DAY

Emil and Emma huddled close around a fire to ward off the morning chill.

Billy returns, carrying the shovel.

> EMIL: Sit down, lad.
>
> BILLY: What happened to breakfast?
>
> EMIL: We'll get to it. I have something to tell you.
>
> EMMA: *We* have something.

Billy, puzzled, sits down.

INT. FAST FOOD JOINT - DAY

Jenny at a table with the two sheriffs, Marti and Don.

>JENNY: Does Billy know his granddad's dying?
>
>MARTI: Nobody knew. He didn't tell anyone.
>
>DEP. HALL: No hint where they might go from the river?
>
>JENNY: I thought they were coming back to Homestead.

EXT. FAST FOOD JOINT - DAY

Jenny seeing off the deputies. Marti and Don stand nearby, waiting.

>JENNY: Will you let me know how Billy is?
>
>DEP. HALL: Sure thing.

INT. FAST FOOD JOINT - DAY

Jenny comes inside.

>YVONNE: Phone, Jenny!

EXT. DESERT TOWN - GAS STATION - DAY

Emil filling the tank.

Billy on a nearby payphone.

INTERCUT

> JENNY: Hello?
>
> BILLY: It's Billy.
>
> JENNY: Where are you?
>
> BILLY: I can't say. I just want you to know I'm okay.
>
> JENNY: Your parents are here. Billy, everyone's worried about your granddad because—
>
> BILLY: I know what's going on. That's why I have to help him.
>
> JENNY: Help him what?
>
> BILLY: I can't say. I just wanted you not to worry. I can't call again until this is over.
>
> JENNY: I was so worried about you.
>
> BILLY: Jenny, I have to run.
>
> JENNY: Billy—
>
> BILLY: I really like you a lot. Bye.

Hanging up, Billy has to catch his breath.

So does Jenny.

EXT. GAS STATION - DAY

Billy returns to the car. Emil hangs up the pump.

> BILLY: I called Jenny. I didn't tell her where we're going or anything.
>
> EMIL: I didn't figure you would. I'm proud that you're willing to help me with this, Billy.

Emma returns from the restroom.

> EMMA: Well. I'm good for a hundred miles, I should think.
>
> EMIL: My turn.

INT. GAS STATION - RESTROOM - DAY

Emil pops a pain pill at the sink. Deep breath.

He looks at himself in the mirror. Pops a second pill.

EXT. DESERT SOUTHWEST - ROAD - DAY

The VW convertible, top down, Billy driving, racing down a country road.

Emil and Emma in the back seat. More serious than before, though. A destination hangs over them.

EXT. MOTEL - NIGHT

The VW parked in front of a motel room.

INT. MOTEL - ROOM - NIGHT

Billy's bag on one bed. On the other, Emil's and Emma's. Obviously they will share a bed.

INT. RESTAURANT - BOOTH - NIGHT

Over dinner in a booth.

Emil makes a sound.

> EMMA: Are you okay?
>
> EMIL: Excuse me.

He gets up and heads for the men's room.

Emma watches him closely.

> EMMA: He's in more pain than he lets on.

Billy is quiet.

INT. RESTAURANT - MEN'S ROOM - NIGHT

Emil at the sink. He pops a pill, then cups his hand for water, chases it down.

He stares at himself in the mirror. He closes his eyes against what he sees.

INT. RESTAURANT - BOOTH - NIGHT

Dessert and coffee.

> EMIL: I've come up with a plan. I don't think you'll like it, so I'm giving you another chance to bail out.
>
> EMMA: I'm not bailing out of anything.
>
> BILLY: Me neither.
>
> EMIL: Better wait till you hear what I have to say.

They wait.

Emil clears his throat. This isn't going to be easy.

INT. MOTEL - NIGHT

Emil pacing.

Billy on the bed, nervous.

The bathroom door closed.

> EMIL: Emma? You're not making matters any easier.

No reply beyond the door.

> EMIL: I shouldn't have told her.

Billy opens his mouth but no words come.

> EMIL: Not you, too. *(to the door)* Emma? I'm going to bed.

Emil goes to his bed. Strips to underwear and crawls in.

Billy still sitting on the bed.

> EMIL: I need to find a good bookstore. There's something you two need to hear.

He turns off his light.

> EMIL: Goodnight.

Billy sits, fighting back tears.

EXT. MOTEL - DAY

Early morning. Emil comes out.

He walks across the lot toward the restaurant.

INT. MOTEL - ROOM - DAY

Billy asleep.

In the other bed, Emma wakes. She realizes Emil is gone.

INT. RESTAURANT - BOOTH - DAY

Emil over coffee, reading the paper.

Emma slips into the booth across from him.

> EMMA: Good morning.
>
> EMIL: Morning.
>
> EMMA: I got it out of my system.
>
> EMIL: I think maybe you should go home.
>
> EMMA: Don't you dare say that. What you're going through is not something a man should do alone. He needs people around who care for him. Billy adores you.

Emil looks at her for the first time.

> EMMA: I adore you.

She offers her hand. He takes it.

The WAITRESS arrives.

> WAITRESS: Don't you two look like you're on your honeymoon?

EXT. MOTEL - DAY

Packing the VW. The top is up.

> EMIL: Billy, you want to start?

Billy gets in behind the wheel. Emil and Emma in back.

EXT. HIGHWAY - DAY

The VW zipping along, top still up.

From the back seat, Emil leans forward and gestures for Billy to take an exit into an approaching town.

EXT. SMALL TOWN - STREET - DAY

The VW is parked on the street.

INT. SMALL TOWN - BOOKSTORE - DAY

Emil rooting around the shelves. He goes to the counter.

> CLERK: May I help you?
>
> EMIL: I surely hope so.

INT. SMALL TOWN - CAFE - DAY

Billy and Emma in a booth.

Emil joins them.

> EMMA: Any luck?
>
> EMIL: Nope. I need a decent bookstore. We'll take a side trip to Boise. It's not too much out of the way.

EXT. HOMESTEAD - SHERIFF'S OFFICE -

DAY

The rental car in front of the small building of the sheriff's office.

INT. SHERIFF'S OFFICE - DAY

Marti and Don meeting with Dep. Hall.

> DEP. HALL: I'm serious. There's nothing you can do here. It may be a day, it might be a week or more. Depends on where they are and how visible they're letting themselves be.
>
> MARTI: We want to be here when you find them.
>
> DEP. HALL: We'll call you immediately. It's up to you.

Marti and Don exchange a glance.

> DON: I do need to check in at work.

INT. AIRPORT - TERMINAL - DAY

Don and Marti in line to board.

> MARTI: What if he's already dead?

Don doesn't reply.

EXT. INTERSTATE - OUTSIDE BOISE - DAY

The VW approaching Boise. Billy driving, top up.

INT. BOISE - BOOKSTORE - DAY

All three in the bookstore. Browsing.

Emil in the Poetry section. Emma down the aisle.

Eureka! He pulls out, "Selected Poems" by Lew Welch.

Behind him, Emma selects something. She approaches Emil.

> EMMA: Look what I found.

She shows Emil a thin volume of poems by Cummings.

EXT. BOOKSTORE - DAY

They exit the bookstore. Emil and Emma each carry a small bag.

EXT. BOISE - MOTEL - NIGHT

The VW parked in the lot of a Boise motel.

INT. MOTEL - ROOM - NIGHT

Emma and Billy sit anxiously at the table.

Emil stands before them, book in hand.

> EMIL: I feel like I'm back in the classroom.

EMMA: I bet you were a wonderful teacher.

EMIL: Flattery will get you everywhere.

He clears his throat.

EMIL: Let me put what I'm going to read in context. Lew Welch was a minor poet among the Beats. Also an alcoholic. So Gary Snyder, a better known poet of the era, lets Welch use his mountain cabin in order to dry out. When Snyder returns to check in on him, Welch is gone. Also gone is the shotgun Snyder kept there. And there's a long poem on the writing desk and in the typewriter. This is the last section of that poem, which is called, "Song of the Turkey Buzzard."

Again he clears his throat. Emma and Billy wait.

EMIL: *(reading)* "Hear my Last Will & Testament: Among my friends there shall always be one with proper instructions for my continuance. Let no one grieve. I shall have used it all up, used up every bit of it. What an extravagance! What a relief! On a marked rock, following his orders, place my meat. All care must be taken not to frighten the natives of this barbarous land, who will not let us die, even, as we wish. With proper ceremony disembowel what I no longer need, that it might more quickly rot and tempt my new form. Not the bronze casket but the brazen wing, soaring forever above thee, o perfect, o sweetest water, o glorious wheeling bird."

Silence.

Emma fights back tears. Billy looks confused.

EMIL: "All care must be taken not to frighten the natives of this barbarous land, who will not let us die, even, as we wish." This part applies directly to me. I know how I want to die. I know the authorities, even my own daughter, would not approve. I've taken you into my trust because I feel you, if not approve, at least will understand what I plan to do. But this is not the time to reveal what. In the morning, we go home to God's country.

BILLY: Are we going back to Homestead?

EMIL: Close.

EXT. RESTAURANT - NIGHT

They come out of the restaurant.

EMMA: *(to Emil)* Let's walk.

EMIL: *(to Billy)* We'll see you back at the motel.

BILLY: Later then.

Billy heads out.

Emil and Emma linger, begin walking in another direction.

EXT. PARK - NIGHT

A small park along the way.

> EMMA: I want to know.
>
> EMIL: This is something I have to do alone.
>
> EMMA: I know that. I just want to be as much a part of you as you'll let me be.
>
> EMIL: I should have married you.
>
> EMMA: No. This is so perfect, it had to happen just this way.

Emil stops and draws her close.

> EMIL: I'm going to the Salmon River out of White Bird. It's where my people come from. I'm going to fish. And then I'm going to end my journey in the river. Don't ask me to say more than this.

They embrace and kiss.

EXT. MOTEL - DAY

Packing up the VW.

> EMIL: I'll drive. One more errand.

EXT. BOISE - MINI-MALL - DAY

Emil parks in a mini-mall.

> EMIL: You two wait for me at Starbucks.
>
> BILLY: Where are you going?
>
> EMIL: I won't be long.

Emil heads out.

> BILLY: *(to Emma)* Do you know what's going on?
>
> EMMA: Let's do as he says.

They head for nearby Starbucks.

EXT. MINI-MALL - GUN SHOP - DAY

Emil enters a gun shop.

INT. GUN SHOP - DAY

Emil is overwhelmed by the variety of weapons he faces.

He wanders around.

Finally he stops at a display of pistols.

EXT. STARBUCKS - OUTDOOR TABLE - DAY

Billy and Emma drink coffee, waiting for Emil.

> BILLY: Here he comes

Across the way, Emil puts something in the car. Then he approaches.

> EMIL: I'm ready when you guys are.

> BILLY: What'd you get?

Emil sits down.

> EMIL: I might as well let you in on this, too, Billy. I bought a gun.

Emma looks away, hit by the reality of the moment.

Billy's expression reveals a slow understanding of Emil's meaning.

> EMIL: The thing is, you have to consider the alternatives. The doctor wanted to put me in a hospice. He means well. He doesn't want me to suffer. But if I'd done that, look at all the adventure we'd have missed. You still wouldn't have caught a fish. For me, this way is better.

> BILLY: For me, too, Gramps.

> EMIL: Good.

He puts his hand on Billy's.

> EMIL: Good.

EXT. INTERSTATE - DAY

Back on the interstate. Billy driving, the top down.

Emil and Emma in back. They sit close, Emil's arm around her.

EXT. INTERSTATE - ANOTHER AREA - DAY

A police car behind the VW turns its lights on.

Billy pulls to the shoulder.

INT./EXT. VW CONVERTIBLE - DAY

Emil turns around, sees the police car pull behind.

> EMIL: Were you speeding?

> BILLY: Unfortunately.

The POLICE OFFICER approaches. He looks at Billy, Emil, Emma.

> POLICE OFFICER: I bet you're Emil Collins.

> EMIL: I am.

> POLICE OFFICER: You've got a lot of

people worried about you, old timer.

INT. RHODES HOUSE - NIGHT

Marti answers the phone.

> MARTI: Hello?...Thank God!

EXT. POLICE STATION - DAY

The VW and police car pull up. Everyone gets out.

A FEMALE OFFICER approaches to lead Emma inside.

Behind them, the officer leads Emil and Billy.

INT. POLICE STATION - ENTRY - DAY

The women move toward one hallway, the men toward another.

> EMMA: Emil, we're jailbirds!
>
> EMIL: Keep your spirits up!
>
> EMMA: Oh, they're up! Up and up and up!

INT. POLICE STATION - CELL - DAY

The police officer leads Emil and Billy to a cell. It's modern and comfortable as far as jails go.

> POLICE OFFICER: Here we go. It ain't the Ritz but there's worse, believe me.

Emil and Billy enter. The officer closes the door behind them.

> EMIL: What time's the cocktail hour?

The officer grins and shakes his head.

> POLICE OFFICER: I thought you were supposed to be sick.

> EMIL: You ought to see me when I'm not.

The officer leaves.

There's a bunk bed against the wall.

> EMIL: You want top or bottom?

> BILLY: Top.

> EMIL: Ever been in jail before?

> BILLY: No way.

> EMIL: Guess you're a jailbird, too. Just don't list this on your college application.

EXT. AIRPORT - NIGHT

A small jetliner lands.

INT. AIRPORT - TERMINAL - NIGHT

Marti and Don enter. They head directly to a car

rental booth.

INT. CELL - NIGHT

Emil and Billy on their bunks. Lights spill into the cell.

In the bottom bunk, Emil pops a pain pill.

> BILLY: Gramps, you awake?
>
> EMIL: I appear to be.
>
> BILLY: What are you going to do now?
>
> EMIL: That is what used to be called the sixty-four thousand dollar question.

EXT. POLICE STATION - DAY

A rental car pulls up, Don behind the wheel. It parks beside the VW.

Marti and Don get out. Don inspects the VW.

> DON: Looks fine.

Marti already heading for the entrance.

INT. POLICE STATION - WAITING ROOM - DAY

Emil, Billy and Emma seated at a long table. The police officer stands.

The door opens, and Marti and Don enter.

> MARTI: Oh, Dad. What am I going to do with you?
>
> EMIL: Too late for talk like that, I'm afraid.
>
> MARTI: You had us worried to death.
>
> EMIL: This is Emma. My daughter, Marti.
>
> EMMA: Hello.
>
> MARTI: Hello.
>
> DON: Hi.
>
> MARTI: Billy. I can't believe you got involved in something like this.
>
> POLICE OFFICER: If I could get some signatures, I can send you folks on your way.

EXT. POLICE STATION - DAY

Emil, Emma, Billy, Marti and Don come out. They stop at the cars. A moment of indecision.

> DON: Somebody has to take Emma back to Homestead. Marti, why don't you do that in the VW and follow us.
>
> EMMA: I'd like to ride with Emil.

> MARTI: I don't think that's a good idea.

> EMIL: Of course it's a good idea. We own the back seat. Come on.

Emil and Emma climb into the back seat of the VW.

Marti stares at Don, as if to say, Do something!

> DON: Billy, guess that leaves you with me.

Marti can't believe her eyes: Don and Billy get into the rental car.

She has no choice but to get behind the wheel of the VW.

The rental car pulls out first. Then the VW.

At the window, the police officer has been watching.

INT. POLICE STATION - WINDOW - DAY

The police officer grins and shakes his head, watching them go.

Another OFFICER passes by.

> POLICE OFFICER: I love that old son-of-a-bitch.

EXT. HIGHWAY - DAY

The caravan heading to Homestead, the rental car in front, the VW behind.

INT. VW CONVERTIBLE - DAY

Marti looks in the rearview mirror. Emil and Emma sitting close. Quiet, content.

Marti looks mentally frazzled.

INT. RENTAL CAR - DAY

Don driving.

> DON: You know he's very sick, don't you?
>
> BILLY: He just wants to die the way he wants to. What's wrong with that?

Don has no answer for him.

EXT. SMALL TOWN - DAY

The cars cruise on Main Street of a small town.

They park in front of a cafe.

INT. CAFE - TABLE - DAY

Around the table with menus. A WAITRESS arrives.

INT. CAFE - TABLE - DAY (LATER)

Empty lunch dishes. Emil is missing.

INT. CAFE - RESTROOM - DAY

Emil at the sink. More pain pills. There aren't many left.

INT. CAFE - TABLE - DAY

Emil returns.

> EMIL: Everything came out okay.
>
> MARTI: Dad, you're incorrigible.
>
> EMIL: There's a big word.
>
> MARTI: You enjoy driving me crazy.
>
> EMIL: You drive yourself crazy.

Marti gets up. Her car keys are on the table.

> MARTI: Excuse me.

She heads for the restroom.

Don picks up the bill.

> DON: Might as well take care of this.

He goes to the cash register, leaving ...

Emil, Emma and Billy alone. Emma leans close to Emil.

> EMMA: *(reciting from memory)* "Since

feeling is first–"

EMIL: *(finishing)* "–who pays any attention to the syntax of things will never wholly kiss you."

They kiss.

EMMA: I'm going to pretend to have a seizure. In the confusion, you two grab the VW and get where you have to get.

BILLY: Gramps, let's do it!

EMIL: My darling Emma.

EMMA: We don't have much time.

EMIL: We'd have to get a different car as soon as possible. There should be a rental agency in the next town, it's large enough.

EMMA: I'll start to the ladies room and collapse on the way. You ready?

EMIL: I should have married you.

EMMA: Quit saying that. Would we be having all this fun now? Here he comes. I'm glad I know you, Mr. Emil Collins. You've brought sunshine into my life.

EMIL: My sweetest Emma.

Don heads back.

Emma gets up and starts to the restroom.

> EMIL: Emma!

She turns. Emil mouths "I love you!" She smiles and continues on.

Marti exits the restroom and comes toward her.

Suddenly Emma falls to the floor.

> MARTI: My God!
>
> DON: *(to waitress)* Somebody call 911!

Marti and Don rush to Emma's side.

Billy grabs the VW keys. He and Emil walk quickly to the door.

EXT. CAFE - DAY

They climb into the VW, Billy behind the wheel. They take off.

INT. CAFE - DAY

Everyone is huddled around Emma.

Suddenly she starts shaking. At first, it appears she might be having a seizure. But in fact she is unable to control her laughter.

Emma becomes a laughing maniac.

Everyone is puzzled. Then Marti looks out the window and notices that the VW is gone.

> MARTI: Don, they're gone!

Don rushes to the window.

> DON: I'll call the police. They won't get far.

EXT. HIGHWAY - DAY

The VW cruising down the highway. Obeying the speed limit.

EXT. HIGHWAY - EXIT - DAY

The VW takes an exit to a town.

EXT. TOWN - RENTAL CAR AGENCY - DAY

The VW parked outside. Billy waiting by the car.

Emil comes out with keys.

> EMIL: We don't want to leave your mother's car here. Makes it too easy for them. We'll park where it'll take a while to find it.

EXT. TOWN - SUPERMARKET - DAY

The new rental car, with Emil driving, enters the parking lot of a supermarket. The VW follows.

Emil gestures for Billy to park. He does.

Emil also parks. He gets out and goes to the VW. Billy climbs out.

Emil opens the passenger door. Then the VW glove compartment. He takes out a pistol.

> EMIL: You drive.
>
> BILLY: You bet.
>
> EMIL: They won't find the car till tomorrow earliest. And that's all the head start we need.
>
> BILLY: Can I hold the gun?
>
> EMIL: Why do you want to do a thing like that?

He hands Billy the pistol anyway.

> BILLY: Is it loaded?
>
> EMIL: Not yet. Let's get out of here.

Billy returns the gun.

They climb into the rental, Billy behind the wheel.

EXT. COUNTRY ROAD - DAY

The rental car on a deserted road.

INT. RENTAL CAR - DAY

Billy still driving.

> EMIL: How you holding up? I can relieve you.
>
> BILLY: I'm not close to tired.
>
> EMIL: Ah, youth!
>
> BILLY: How far before we stop?
>
> EMIL: Well, if you don't mind driving, we could get there tonight.
>
> BILLY: Let's do it.

EXT. COUNTRY STORE - NIGHT

The rental car pulls up to a country store.

INT. RENTAL CAR - NIGHT

Billy, behind the wheel, starts to get out. Emil touches him.

> EMIL: This is where I get off.

Billy looks confused.

> EMIL: I want you to drive back to Homestead and turn yourself in.
>
> BILLY: Why?

EMIL: This is the end of the line.

BILLY: But you were going fishing.

EMIL: There's a trail behind the store. Leads right to the river.

BILLY: You don't have a pole, bait, nothing.

EMIL: There's fishing and then there's fishing.

Billy looks on the verge of tears.

EMIL: Sometimes when I'm fishing, I wish I had no bait on the hook because the last thing I want is a bite. It would spoil the serenity of the moment. It would spoil another kind of fishing I'm doing out there.

BILLY: I don't get it.

EMIL: Sometimes I'm out on the river for ... what's the word? Understanding. An understanding of myself. When you get to be my age, you'll get it fine.

A silence.

BILLY: What do I tell mom?

EMIL: That you're the best grandson a fella could have. You give me respect, Billy. This

> whole trip, you gave me nothing but respect. I couldn't ask for anything more from you. I love you, lad.
>
> BILLY: I love you, Gramps.

Now the tears come.

> BILLY: I'm sorry.

He takes out a handkerchief, tries to get himself under control.

> EMIL: Never apologize for feeling deeply. Now I want you to do one last thing for me.
>
> BILLY: Okay.
>
> EMIL: Your mother's going to get her way in the end. They'll find me, they'll be a funeral and a lot of nice speeches and the rest. And then I'll get the bronze casket. That's fine. But while you're watching me go six feet under, look around and see if you can see a bird in the sky. That's where my spirit will be. On "the brazen wing." And I couldn't have done this without you, lad.

Emil gives Billy a hug.

Emil gets out. He leans into the window.

> EMIL: You drive safely now. Go on. I want to see you driving down the road.

Billy nods. He backs up. The VW moves back down the road.

Emil watches till the car is out of sight.

EXT. RIVER - NIGHT

A quiet peaceful spot along the river. A bright moon overhead throws light onto the water.

Emil sits on a stump overlooking the river. He holds the pistol.

A bald eagle in a tree. Silence.

A deer in the brush. Silence.

The moon, almost full. Magical.

Suddenly: BANG.

The deer scurries into the brush.

The eagle takes flight.

The stump along the river is vacant.

EXT. CEMETERY - DAY

MOURNERS at Emil's grave site. Family and friends, including Wally.

The bronze casket being lowered into the ground.

In front, with his parents, is Billy. In a dark suit.

Somber.

He looks up. He searches the sky and ...

...there it is! A bird gliding on the air currents.

A magnificent, glorious, wheeling bird!

> EMIL (V.O.): "Not the bronze casket but the brazen wing, soaring forever above thee, o perfect, o sweetest water, o glorious wheeling bird."

A smile comes to Billy's lips.

FADE OUT

CASANOVA DOES CALIFORNIA

An irate father gives the historic Casanova a magic potion that propels him to present day Venice, California, where he is appalled by his historic reputation, shocked by a porno movie being made about him, and falls in love with the psychiatrist who evaluates his sanity.

FADE IN:

SUPER

"Venice, Italy. Summer, 1749."

EXT. VENICE - COUNTRY VILLA - NIGHT

A second-story window is lit by a lantern. Below, hidden behind trees, wait three men: these are LORENZO LEBANO, whose home it is, and two of his workers, VENNY and GIOVANNI.

Two figures become a silhouette at the window, a MAN and WOMAN in a passionate embrace. Lorenzo hisses the name of his daughter.

> LORENZO: Rosabel!

Venny and Giovanni comfort him.

> GIOVANNI: He will pay for this.

The window opens and the man climbs out and grabs the branch of an adjacent tree. This is Giacomo Girolamo CASANOVA, 20s, handsome, athletic, dashing. He wears the frills of an 18th century gentleman.

From the window ROSABEL, a teenager, blows him a kiss and disappears. Below, Lorenzo makes a soft sound of anguish. Giovanni and Venny sneak forward to do their work.

Casanova shimmies down the tree. Giovanni and Venny are waiting for him. They grab him, and Casanova struggles.

Rosabel comes again to the window and sees what is happening.

> ROSABEL: Casanova!

Her father steps forward to shout up at her, shaking his fist.

> LORENZO: How ashamed your mother would be of you!

Giovanni and Venny have Casanova under control. They gag and bind him, then drag him off to follow Lorenzo.

> ROSABEL: Father, let him go, I love him! Casanova, I love you!

INT. COUNTRY VILLA - SHED - NIGHT

A lantern casts eerie shadows in a workshed. Casanova sits in a chair, still bound and gagged.

Lorenzo takes a vial from a shelf and shakes it. He glares at Casanova.

> LORENZO: You have a reputation for performing great feats of magic. Now we'll

see how well you take your own medicine. *(to the workers)* Remove the gag.

Giovanni removes the gag. Casanova quickly pleads.

> CASANOVA: I am willing to marry your daughter.
>
> LORENZO: How dare you make such a suggestion! You, the son of actors! You are scum! *(to the workers)* Hold his nose and open his mouth.

They do so, and Lorenzo forces Casanova to drink the liquid in the vial.

Casanova coughs, clears his throat.

> LORENZO: In the nether world, you won't be such a lover.
>
> CASANOVA: My reputation is greatly exaggerated. If you'd let me explain–

Lorenzo steps forward and strikes Casanova, knocking him cold.

> LORENZO: Farewell, Giacomo Casanova. May God have mercy on your soul. *(to the others)* Get him out of here.

SUPER

"Venice, California. Summer, the Present."

EXT. VENICE - PROMENADE - DAY

Ocean Front Walk on a weekend.

A Promenade is lined with palm trees and stretches along the sand for miles. Elbow-to-elbow PEDESTRIANS wearing California casual move through a carnival-like atmosphere.

EXT. VENICE - BEACH - DAY

Casanova, wearing the same 18th century frills of a gentleman, lies on the sand. He appears to be asleep – or worse.

BIKINI-CLAD MEN AND WOMEN pass by, giving him hardly a notice. On this beach, in this town, at this time, the sight of a strangely-dressed man passed out on the sand is no cause for alarm.

Casanova stirs. He opens his eyes. He manages to sit up. He looks around.

Shock. He blinks and looks around again. He might as well be on another planet – in a way he is! – for all the sense he can make of what he sees.

Nearly naked men and women continue to pass by him. They smile, they chat – but to Casanova, they are aliens. It's as if he is being assaulted by bare navels, exposed breasts, tight buttocks.

INT. VENICE, ITALY - COUNTRY VILLA - NIGHT - (MEMORY FLASH)

As Casanova crawls in the bedroom window, Rosabel starts unlacing the front of her dress.

> CASANOVA: Stop it, Rosabel. You deny me the pleasure of doing it myself.

> ROSABEL: But there's so little time!

> CASANOVA: A woman's greatest attraction is her modesty. The journey must be as pleasurable as the destination.

EXT. VENICE, CALIF. - BEACH - DAY (PRESENT)

Two especially lovely YOUNG WOMEN pass by, their bikinis revealing everything. Casanova still sits on the sand, stunned by his surroundings.

> FIRST YOUNG WOMAN: Hey, dude, nice rags!

> SECOND YOUNG WOMAN: Cool, Casanova!

The sound of his name floors him. His eyes dart around in confusion.

He sees the Promenade along the beach and heads for it.

EXT. VENICE - SIDE STREET - DAY

A van pulls over to drop passengers off. On the side

of the van is written "Los Angeles County. Department of Mental Health."

Getting out is DR. HENNY THOMAS, 30s, and four PATIENTS. Before closing the door, Henny talks to the driver.

> HENNY: Pick us up here in two hours.

She gathers up the patients and gets them walking in a group toward the Promenade ahead.

EXT. VENICE - PROMENADE - DAY

Casanova hurries along the busy Promenade, oblivious to the sauntering, sweating mass of humanity surrounding him: pedestrians, bicyclists, skateboarders, roller bladers. He slices through the weekend crowd like a man who is lost and confused.

Someone hands him a flier. It reads: "Discover the Goddess Energy! Classes start soon!"

He passes an area of beach full of weight lifters; another where people play table tennis.

Along the Promenade, vendors sell T-shirts and hot dogs, sun glasses and tarot cards.

There are street musicians and sidewalk preachers, portrait artists and jugglers.

Casanova continues moving, a man desperate to get anywhere but here.

Another flier is shoved at him. "Unhappy Sex Life? HOLISTIC ORGASMS RELEASE THE UNIVERSAL EROS!!"

A little farther along, Casanova passes a MOTHER who is helping her BOY, who has a nose bleed. She has a handkerchief at his nose.

> MOTHER: Tilt your head back.

Casanova stares at the boy.

INT. VENICE, ITALY - ROOM - DAY (MEMORY FLASH)

YOUNG CASANOVA's head is tilted back, just like the boy's. His MOTHER holds a cloth to his nose.

> CASANOVA'S MOTHER: Giacomo, you are such a sickly boy. Every day your nose bleeds. What am I going to do with you?

EXT. VENICE - PROMENADE - DAY (PRESENT)

Henny leads her patients down the Promenade. Coming in the other direction is Casanova.

A TEENAGED BOY on a skateboard grabs Henny's purse as he zooms by.

> HENNY: Hey! Thief, thief!

The teenager practically runs over Casanova as he

passes. Henny is pointing at the fleeing kid and yelling.

Casanova reacts quickly, turning and racing after the thief.

A SERIES OF SHOTS - THE CHASE

The teenager moves off the Promenade onto a bicycle path. Casanova races after him.

Pedestrians move out of the way of the teenager, who is speeding recklessly on his skateboard and putting distance between himself and Casanova.

The path begins a broad sweeping turn, and Casanova runs off the path to cut across in a shortcut.

The teenager and Casanova reach a straight-away on the path at the same time. Casanova tackles the kid, and they both fall to the ground.

The skateboard and Henny's purse go flying. Casanova recovers first and jumps on the boy.

But the boy wiggles free. He grabs a handful of sand and throws it in Casanova's face.

By the time Casanova recovers, the boy is skating off again. The purse lies on the ground.

Casanova lets him go and picks up the purse.

EXT. VENICE - PROMENADE - DAY

Casanova presents Henny with her purse.

> HENNY: Thank you so much.

Casanova, exhausted, bows low.

Henny's patients are taken by Casanova's costume. They can't hide their amusement.

> HENNY: Let me pay you for your trouble.
>
> CASANOVA: It is never trouble to come to the assistance of a beautiful woman.

This is the first time we've heard Casanova talk, and he speaks a more formal English than natives do. This also is the last thing Henny expected to hear. She's flustered, taken off-guard.

Henny's patients are beginning to wander off.

> HENNY: Stay together, people!

She gathers them back in, then turns back to Casanova.

> HENNY: I don't know how to thank you.

But while her back was turned, Casanova moved off. She can't find him in the crowd.

EXT. VENICE - PROMENADE - DAY - LATER

Casanova continues down the Prominade.

>CHRISTIANO: *(O.S.)* Giacomo!

Hearing his name, Casanova looks puzzled.

CHRISTIANO, 20s, appears. He wears shorts, sandals and a bright T-shirt, looking like a native.

>CHRISTIANO: Giacomo? It's me, Christiano.

He pulls Casanova aside, out of the throng of moving people.

>CHRISTIANO: Don't you recognize me?

>CASANOVA: Christiano?

>CHRISTIANO: You look terrible. You just got here, didn't you?

>CASANOVA: Where am I?

>CHRISTIANO: America. It's far beyond Marco Polo's wildest dreams!

>CASANOVA: Why am I speaking English? I don't know English.

>CHRISTIANO: You do now. But still thinking in Italian, right?

Casanova nods, looking very confused.

CHRISTIANO: I can't tell you what a relief it is to find someone else from home.

CASANOVA: How long have you been here?

CHRISTIANO: About six months. Remember Lorenzo Lebano? I was climbing through his daughter's window every night. It was so sweet while it lasted. Then I got caught, he forced me to drink a magic potion – and here I am!

CASANOVA: You and Rosabel?

CHRISTIANO: Don't tell me ... but, of course, it makes perfect sense! Sweet Rosabel. I missed her for almost a week.

CASANOVA: I want to go home.

CHRISTIANO: I'm working on it. In the meantime, this is an amazing place, Giacomo, you won't believe how people behave here. There's so much to tell you, I don't know where to begin. You must be starving.

CASANOVA: I am very hungry.

CHRISTIANO: I found a place that makes wonderful pasta. My treat. In a few days, after you've had time to adjust, you can help me follow some leads.

CASANOVA: Leads?

CHRISTIANO: A couple people we need to talk to. We've got to find the magic that will get us back.

CASANOVA: As soon as possible! I belong in Italy.

CHRISTIANO: Italy's the easy part. It's getting back to our own time that's the bitch. Are you ready for this? Here it's the twenty-first century.

CASANOVA: I belong in 1749, I belong in Venice.

CHRISTIANO: This is Venice – California!

CASANOVA: I do not understand.

CHRISTIANO: Come on, you'll think more clearly on a full stomach.

EXT. VENICE - PROMENADE - PUBLIC RESTROOM - DAY

They pass a public restroom.

CHRISTIANO: I gotta pee.

Christiano enters and Casanova, hesitating a moment, follows him.

INT. PUBLIC RESTROOM - DAY

Christiano goes to a urinal. Casanova waits behind, wide-eyed, not sure what kind of building he's entered.

Christiano finally notices Casanova's wonder.

> CHRISTIANO: Isn't this incredible?

He flushes and zips up.

> CHRISTIANO: Wait'll you see this.

He opens a door and presents the toilet.

> CHRISTIANO: For the bowels.

He flushes it. Casanova stares at the circling water.

> CASANOVA: Where does it go?

Christiano shrugs off the question.

> CHRISTIANO: Not in the street! Everyone here is obsessed with cleanliness. Come on.

He leads the way out. With a final look around in amazement, Casanova hurries behind him.

EXT. VENICE - ANGELO'S CAFE - DAY

They sit outside at a sidewalk cafe. Casanova is wolfing down a large plate of pasta like he hasn't eaten in days. Christiano sips a glass of red wine.

> CHRISTIANO: First, we've got to get you a

place to stay tonight. And a way to make some spare change. You played in the orchestra ... if we can get you a violin, you'll do fine. You can be a street musician. Tonight, anyway, you can crash at the shelter, long as we get there early enough to reserve you a cot. I've been crashing at the studio. I've making a movie.

CASANOVA: What is that?

CHRISTIANO: You won't believe your eyes. Movies are the best thing here. What I'm doing is just a low budget thing – it's either erotica or porno, depending on whether you're for or against it.

CASANOVA: Porno?

CHRISTIANO: I get paid for making love to women. I don't know how to tell you this, but you're in the title. "Casanova Does California."

CASANOVA: I do not understand.

CHRISTIANO: You won't believe the reputation you have here. You're considered the greatest lover of all time. Listen, I may be able to get you a small part. Hell, maybe Tom will even let you crash at the studio. We'll stop by on our way to the shelter.

EXT. VENICE - PROMENADE - DAY

Henny window-shops with her patients. She keeps a close watch on them.

EXT. VENICE - BUSINESS AREA - DAY

Casanova and Christiano are away from the beach, walking along a sidewalk in a business area. Many of the buildings have flashy murals painted on them.

>CHRISTIANO: The thing is, if you say you're Casanova, eventually you'll get locked up for being crazy. You can't tell the truth here.
>
>CASANOVA: I always tell the truth.
>
>CHRISTIANO: I tried to tell the truth in the beginning, too, and I ended up in jail. I'm still seeing a shrink as part of my parole. Believe me, it's an experience you want to avoid.
>
>CASANOVA: Who am I if I am not who I am?
>
>CHRISTIANO: I'll call you Amado. You're my cousin visiting from Venice in the old country. Let me do the talking. This way.

They turn on a side street.

EXT. VENICE - SIDE STREET - DAY

They continue walking. Ahead, a small group of

WOMEN are picketing in front of a windowless, square building.

The women carry signs reading things like "Tom Snow Productions Debases Women!," "No Porno in Venice!," and "Casanova Does Life Without Parole!"

> CHRISTIANO: Oh shit, they're here again. We'll have to use the back entrance.

Christiano leads the way into an alley, circling around to the back of the building.

INT. TOM SNOW PRODUCTIONS - OFFICE - DAY

TOM SNOW, 50s, sits behind a huge desk. He's a short stocky man who looks older than he is. His face looks like it's been hit by an avalanche.

Snow's eyes are closed. He is making little groaning sounds. At first, it's hard to know what he's up to.

Then his eyes snap open, his chin drops, the groan becomes louder and more sustained, and he grimaces. With a final gasp, he is done.

He clears his throat and pushes back his chair. He reaches down to zip up his fly.

Popping up from under the desk is SYLVIA, 20s, his secretary.

> TOM: Thanks, honey, that was really great.

> SYLVIA: Thank you, Mr. Snow.

> TOM: Don't forget to note it on your time sheet.

> SYLVIA: Anything else?

> TOM: Put on the tape of dailies before you go.

INT. TOM SNOW PRODUCTIONS - FRONT DESK - DAY

Christiano leads Casanova into the office. The front desk is empty.

> CHRISTIANO: Anybody home!

Sylvia quickly appears.

> SYLVIA: Hi, Chris. You want to see Tom?

> TOM: *(O.S.)* Chris, get your ass in here!

INT. TOM SNOW PRODUCTIONS - OFFICE - DAY

Tom is watching a VIDEO TAPE, where Christiano and Sylvia are on an ornate bed, in a passionate embrace. Christiano is dressed like Casanova, in 18th century frills.

Christiano and Casanova enter.

> TOM: This scene sucks. It takes too

goddamn long for everybody to get naked.

For the first time he spins away from the TV.

> TOM: Who's this?
>
> CHRISTIANO: My cousin, Amado. He's just come over from the old country.
>
> TOM: How about a drink?

Without waiting for an answer, Tom swings his chair around to the full bar behind him.

Casanova can't keep his eyes off the moving images on the TV. He approaches the set and looks behind it, trying to understand how it works, where the images come from.

Tom notices this.

> TOM: Something wrong?
>
> CHRISTIANO: Amado, what's the matter, you never seen a TV before? Your village isn't that primitive!

He laughs like crazy and pushes Casanova into a chair.

INT. TOM SNOW PRODUCTIONS - OFFICE - DAY - LATER

A nearly empty bottle of Scotch is on the desk. Tom has been holding court.

> TOM: It's the image, it's always the image! Fucking writers never know that. All they know is words. Show me a writer and I'll show you too many goddamn words!

Sylvia sticks her head in the doorway.

> SYLVIA: I'm leaving now, Mr. Snow.

> TOM: Wait a minute.

He leans over the desk and grins.

> TOM: Amado, you want to get a little head before she goes? She's great, trust me.

Casanova, not sure what has been asked, shoots a puzzling look to Christiano.

> CHRISTIANO: *(to change the subject)* Tom, I forgot to tell you, the picketers are outside again.

> TOM: Goddamn ice queens. Somebody should fuck their brains out and give them a life.

> SYLVIA: Maybe I'd better go out the back way. If that's all right ...

> TOM: Amado, you want some?

Casanova shrugs, still confused.

TOM: Get out of here, honey. See you in the morning.

INT. TOM SNOW PRODUCTIONS - BASEMENT - DAY

A dark basement. A LIGHT snaps on.

Tom leads Christiano and Casanova down a stairway into the basement. Casanova, taking up the rear, moves with hesitation.

INT. VENICE, ITALY - STAIRWAY/BASEMENT - DAY (MEMORY FLASH)

Casanova's mother waits at the foot of the stairs as the boy slowly comes down, step by careful step. The basement is dark, cast in shadows from a lantern.

> CASANOVA'S MOTHER: Hurry up, Giacomo! You want your nose bleeds to stop or not?

The boy reaches the bottom. An OLD WOMAN comes forward, appearing haggard, scary, maybe a gypsy, maybe a witch.

> OLD WOMAN: Bring the boy this way.

Casanova's mother takes his hand, and they follow the old woman to a seaman's trunk. The old woman raises the lid.

> OLD WOMAN: Put the boy in the chest.
>
> CASANOVA: No, mama!
>
> CASANOVA'S MOTHER: Do as she says, Giacomo. This is going to stop your nose bleeds.

The mother and old woman together get the boy into the trunk.

> OLD WOMAN: Hold him down.

The mother holds him down while the woman sprinkles herbs over him.

> OLD WOMAN: Let him go.

As soon as the mother's arms are out of the way, the old woman slams down the lid with Casanova inside.

> CASANOVA'S MOTHER: How long must he be inside?
>
> OLD WOMAN: As long as it takes.

INT. TOM SNOW PRODUCTIONS - BASEMENT - DAY (PRESENT)

Casanova reaches the bottom of the stairs and comes into the room.

The basement is a movie set. The ornate bed from the dailies is along a wall, the focus of an array of movie lights.

In a corner, a sleeping bag is rolled out over a mattress.

> TOM: Amado, you got a sleeping bag?
>
> CHRISTIANO: I know where I can borrow one.
>
> TOM: It's all yours then.
>
> CHRISTIANO: Really appreciate this, Tom.
>
> TOM: I've got to get out of here. It's the old lady's birthday.

He starts back up the stairs.

> CHRISTIANO: See you in the morning.

Tom is gone.

> CASANOVA: This is where you sleep?
>
> CHRISTIANO: It's not as bad as it looks. And the price is right. Come on, we've got to get you a sleeping bag. And a violin. And some clothes.

INT. VENICE - PROMENADE - DAY

Casanova and Christiano come out of a sporting goods store. Casanova is wearing shorts, sandals, a tank top and a baseball cap. He carries his native clothes in a paper bag.

> CHRISTIANO: Now the violin, the sleeping bag, and we're done.
>
> HENNY: Hello, Chris.

Christiano turns to find Henny and her patients.

> HENNY: *(to Casanova)* Hello again.
>
> CHRISTIANO: You know each other?
>
> HENNY: *(ignoring this)* Didn't you have an appointment to see me this morning?
>
> CHRISTIANO: Did I? God, I can't believe I missed it. Did you–
>
> HENNY: I haven't told your parole officer. Yet. Will I see you in the morning?
>
> CHRISTIANO: I got this job ... but, sure, I can work something out. Can we make it eight?
>
> HENNY: That's a little early, isn't it?
>
> CHRISTIANO: I wouldn't have to miss much work that way.
>
> HENNY: Eight it is.

She turns her focus to Casanova, who is staring at her. In fact, Casanova appears to be mesmerized by her.

Henny offers her hand. Casanova starts shaking it and doesn't let go.

> HENNY: I'm Henny Thomas. Thank you again. *(to Christiano)* He stopped a thief from stealing my purse.
>
> CHRISTIANO: Really?
>
> HENNY: *(to Casanova)* You never told me your name.
>
> CHRISTIANO: *(quickly)* This is my cousin Amado from the old country.
>
> HENNY: Are you visiting long?

Casanova pulls her hand forward, bends down, and kisses it. A slow gentle kiss that leaves Henny speechless.

> CASANOVA: You have extraordinary eyes.

Christiano pulls Casanova away and starts hurrying off. As they depart, he talks over his shoulder.

> CHRISTIANO: Nice running into you, and I'll be at your office at eight! Thanks for not reporting me! It won't happen again!

Henny looks puzzled, watching them go. She holds up the hand that was kissed and stares at it.

She discovers that her patients have strayed and quickly gets into gear to round them up.

Christiano drags Casanova along.

> CHRISTIANO: Forget about getting her purse, she's not available.

EXT. TOM SNOW PRODUCTIONS - NIGHT

The building is deserted, the picketers long gone. No visible lights are on.

INT. TOM SNOW PRODUCTIONS - BASEMENT - NIGHT

Christiano is sprawled across his sleeping bag, reading a script, memorizing his lines.

A second mattress has been pulled near his. Casanova sits on a sleeping bag, tuning a violin.

With the instrument in tune, Casanova tries it out. He plays something classical from the 18th century.

> CHRISTIANO: Man, you're gonna wow the shit out of the tourists. They're not used to hearing classical out there.

Casanova sets down the violin.

> CHRISTIANO: Help me with lines.

He tosses Casanova his script.

CHRISTIANO: Scene 43. I'm Casanova, you're Honey Buns.

CASANOVA: Why are you pretending to be me?

CHRISTIANO: Not the real Casanova, it's my part in the picture. I told you, they think of you as history's great superstud. Scene 43, the first line is yours.

CASANOVA: *(reading)* "I can suck chrome off a bumper." What does this mean?

CHRISTIANO: *(reciting his lines)* "You can use my bumper any time, baby. I got more hot meat for you than a Coney Island chili dog stand."

EXT. TOM SNOW PRODUCTIONS - NIGHT

Casanova storms out of the building. A moment later Christiano comes out.

He catches up with him.

CHRISTIANO: Giacomo, you don't get it. It doesn't matter if it doesn't make any sense. These kind of movies, people watch them with the sound off till everybody gets naked. Then it's all background music and heavy breathing.

CASANOVA: What you said is an insult to lovemaking!

Christiano stops and lets him go.

>CHRISTIANO: *(after him)* You gonna be able to find your way back?

No answer.

EXT. VENICE - PROMENADE - NIGHT

Casanova walks along the Promenade. It's much less crowded than during the day.

He approaches a restaurant as Henny comes out with TED MINER, 40s. She recognizes Casanova.

>HENNY: Amado? Nice to see you again.

Casanova also recognizes her and bows low in her honor.

>HENNY: I'd like you to meet my fiancee, Ted Miner.

>TED: Hello.

He offers his hand. Casanova gives only a single shake.

>HENNY: *(to Ted)* Amado's the one I was telling you about. He's visiting from Italy.

>TED: Rome?

>CASANOVA: Venice.

TED: Which do you prefer, Venice, Italy or Venice, California?

CASANOVA: I miss my home.

HENNY: Already? *(to Ted)* He just got here.

CASANOVA: Why are you marrying him?

HENNY: Excuse me?

CASANOVA: He is not the man you should marry. It would be a great mistake if you do this.

TED: *(to Henny)* You sure he isn't one of your patients?

HENNY: Well, Amado, it doesn't really matter what you think, does it? Have a pleasant evening.

She grabs Ted's hand and heads off. Casanova watches them go, growing concern in his gaze.

EXT. VENICE - STREET - NIGHT

Casanova walks along a sidewalk, trying to recognize where he is. In fact, he is lost.

A WOMAN PEDESTRIAN approaches from the other direction. Seeing Casanova, she crosses the street.

He also crosses the street, and they approach one another again.

She crosses back. He crosses back.

She takes something out of her purse and stops.

> WOMAN PEDESTRIAN: I have Mace!

He keeps walking toward her.

> CASANOVA: Excuse me! Can you help me? I am terribly lost.
>
> WOMAN PEDESTRIAN: What's the address?
>
> CASANOVA: I wish I knew.

He reaches her.

> CASANOVA: The name is Tom Snow Productions.
>
> WOMAN PEDESTRIAN: Pervert!

The woman lets out a sudden screech and sprays him with Mace.

EXT. VENICE - PROMENADE - NIGHT

Casanova is at a water fountain, rinsing out his eyes. While he's still blinded, two TEENAGERS come up to him.

TEENAGER #1: Give me your wallet.

The second teenager snaps open a switchblade.

TEENAGER #2: Now, motherfucker!

Casanova still can't see clearly.

TEENAGER #2: *(to the other)* Get it!

The first teenager grabs for Casanova's wallet. Casanova grasps his arm, twists it, and drops the boy to the ground.

The other teenager jumps on his back but Casanova bends forward, throwing him to the ground as well.

The teenagers have had enough and scramble to their feet, running off.

Casanova rubs his eyes, the Mace still having its effect.

EXT. VENICE - STREET - NIGHT

Henny is cleaning Casanova's face with a damp handkerchief. Ted leans against his convertible at the curb.

HENNY: I'm so glad we passed by and saw you. This is such a terrible thing to happen on your first night in America. Please don't think we're all like those hoodlums. How are you doing? Feel better?

CASANOVA: This feels very nice.

HENNY: Good. Can we give you a ride somewhere?

CASANOVA: Tom Snow Productions.

HENNY: Why does that ring a bell? Do you know the address?

EXT. VENICE - PAY PHONE - NIGHT

The convertible is parked near a pay phone. Ted is looking in the yellow pages.

TED: Got it.

EXT. TOM SNOW PRODUCTIONS - NIGHT

The convertible pulls up in front of the dark building.

INT. CONVERTIBLE - NIGHT

Casanova sits alone in back. Henny swings around to face him.

HENNY: Is anybody here?

CASANOVA: Christiano and I sleep in the basement.

HENNY: I thought he was staying at a halfway house. Interesting.

Casanova gets out.

EXT. TOM SNOW PRODUCTIONS – CONVERTIBLE - NIGHT

He goes to Henny's side. He offers his hand. When she offers hers, he bends low and kisses it again.

> TED: Amado, how do you like California so far?
>
> CASANOVA: *(reciting a poem)* "Midway in our life's journey, I went astray / from the straight road and woke to find myself / alone in a dark wood. How shall I say // what wood that was! I never saw so dreary, / so rank, so arduous a wilderness! / Its very memory gives a shape to fear."

He stops and glares at Ted.

> HENNY: Is that something you wrote?
>
> CASANOVA: Alighieri wrote it.
>
> HENNY: I don't know him.
>
> CASANOVA: Dante Alighieri is our best poet.
>
> HENNY: Oh, Dante! I didn't realize he was world-famous by his first name! Did you know that, Ted?

Ted has had enough of this nonsense and puts the

car in gear, laying rubber to get away from there.

INT. TOM SNOW PRODUCTIONS - BASEMENT - NIGHT

Casanova comes downstairs. Christiano has fallen asleep while reading.

Casanova turns out the light next to Christiano. He crawls into his own sleeping bag and gets comfortable.

He looks at the ceiling, thinking.

INT. VENICE, ITALY - BASEMENT - DAY (MEMORY FLASH)

The old woman opens the seaman's trunk. Casanova's mother watches.

Even though there is only lantern light in the basement, the young Casanova squints, blinded. He sits up.

> OLD WOMAN: No nose bleed.
>
> CASANOVA'S MOTHER: Is he cured?
>
> OLD WOMAN: We'll have to wait and see.

EXT. VENICE - PROMENADE - DAY (PRESENT)

Christiano helps Casanova get settled at a spot along the Promenade.

Outside a shop nearby, the OWNER is sweeping. He stops to watch with curiosity as Casanova, wearing his new beach attire, gets ready to play the violin.

Christiano arranges the open violin case, then takes out a dollar and drops it in.

> CHRISTIANO: Seed money. I'll see my shrink, go to work and when we're done shooting, I'll come by to see how you're making out. You gonna be all right?
>
> CASANOVA: Such a beautiful day! I will play beautiful music.
>
> CHRISTIANO: That's the spirit.

Christiano heads out. Before he's far, Casanova begins a classical piece. Christiano grins.

People along the Promenade gather to watch Casanova.

A street performer, a SWORD SWALLOWER, watches his audience disperse to listen to the beautiful violin music.

INT. HENNY'S OFFICE - DAY

Christiano sits across the desk from Henny.

> HENNY: I ran into Amado last night.

CHRISTIANO: Really?

HENNY: He says he's staying with you – but not at the halfway house. We dropped him off.

CHRISTIANO: It's just temporary, for convenience. It's where my job is and we like to start early in the morning.

HENNY: You haven't told me about this job. What is it?

CHRISTIANO: It's, ah, you know, an acting job.

HENNY: Acting! I didn't know you were an actor.

CHRISTIANO: Just a small role, you know, nothing very important.

HENNY: A film or a play or ... ?

CHRISTIANO: No, it's, ah, you know, an instructional video.

HENNY: Very good.

INT. HENNY'S OFFICE - FRONT DESK - DAY

Henny walks Christiano out of the office.

HENNY: Are you showing Amado the

sights?

CHRISTIANO: I left him playing the violin on Ocean Front.

HENNY: He's a street musician?

CHRISTIANO: Gives him something to do while I'm working.

HENNY: Interesting.

EXT. VENICE - PROMENADE - DAY

Casanova plays the violin. Quite a crowd has gathered to listen.

The nearby Sword Swallower glares at the new competition. He packs up and moves on in disgust.

INT. TOM SNOW PRODUCTIONS - BASEMENT - DAY

Tom stands next to the ornate bed, where Christiano and Sylvia are nude under flimsy "between takes" robes. A camera is behind him, and bright lights glare down on the bed.

TOM: The sequence is, you do a sixty-nine, then you sit up on top of him, facing the camera, and you reach around and grab her tits. I want lots of squealing.

EXT. VENICE - PROMENADE - DAY

Casanova plays the violin. The crowd is even larger. In it is Henny.

Great applause when Casanova finishes. Many people move forward to drop change or bills into the violin case.

Casanova is about to begin another piece when he notices Henny, who has moved to the front of the line.

>CASANOVA: Hello!

>HENNY: Hi. Can I buy you lunch when you take a break?

>CASANOVA: Look how well I am doing! Let me buy you lunch.

>HENNY: In about an hour?

>CASANOVA: Good.

>HENNY: Go straight down the Promenade and on the left you'll run into Cupid's Retreat.

>CASANOVA: A good name!

He begins playing a passionate, gypsy-sounding piece.

EXT. CUPID'S RETREAT - PATIO - DAY

Casanova finds Henny at a table. He hurries over,

bows low and sits.

> CASANOVA: I feel like I met you in a previous life.
>
> HENNY: Really?
>
> CASANOVA: Your soul feels so familiar to me.
>
> HENNY: And if I don't believe in previous lives?
>
> CASANOVA: But I am living proof that they exist.
>
> HENNY: How's that?

He scoots his chair closer to her.

> CASANOVA: My name is not Amado. I am Giacomo Casanova. The day before yesterday, by my senses, I was forced to drink a magic potion on a summer night in Venice, Italy, in 1749. When I came to, I was on the beach here, and Christiano tells me this is the twenty-first century!

Henny narrows her gaze at him.

> CASANOVA: I think we met in 1749. I feel like I know you.
>
> HENNY: A street musician, a weaver of tall tales – you have many talents.

CASANOVA: Do you believe me?

HENNY: Of course I don't believe you.

She laughs.

HENNY: You also butt into matters that don't concern you. Ted was very upset by your remark last night. I wouldn't marry him if he wasn't the right man.

CASANOVA: No, you are making a terrible mistake!

HENNY: Amado–

CASANOVA: Casanova.

HENNY: Amado–

CASANOVA: Casanova!

A WAITER appears.

WAITER: Are you ready to order?

Henny stands up.

HENNY: I'm sorry. I'm not as hungry as I thought I was.

She marches away. Casanova is not sure what to do under the circumstances.

CASANOVA: Then I am not hungry either. Am I supposed to pay you for your trouble?

WAITER: If you like.

Casanova tips him far too much and takes off after Henny. The waiter shakes his head and grins.

EXT. VENICE - PROMENADE - DAY

Casanova catches up with Henny.

CASANOVA: Why are you upset?

HENNY: I don't like to be played for a sucker. Amado!

CASANOVA: If it makes you feel better, you can call me Amado.

HENNY: How noble of you.

CASANOVA: You must still be hungry. We can go somewhere else.

She stops and stares at him.

HENNY: No! I made a mistake coming here to see you. I don't know what I was thinking. I want you to stop following me.

Henny is quickly gone, and Casanova is crushed.

He turns to find a JUGGLER controlling three chain saws in the air.

Someone hands him a flier that says, "Lose 30 pounds in 30 days!"

EXT. VENICE - PROMENADE - DAY - LATER

Casanova plays a classical tear-jerker on the violin. He really gets into it, tears welling in his eyes.

INT. VENICE, ITALY - DRAWING ROOM - DAY (MEMORY FLASH)

The young Casanova is playing the same melody on a smaller violin, giving a concert in a drawing room.

A guest whispers to Casanova's mother.

> GUEST: He has so much talent. How is his health?
>
> CASANOVA'S MOTHER: No nose bleeds in over a year.

INT. TOM SNOW PRODUCTIONS - BASEMENT - DAY (PRESENT)

Tom films the sex action on the bed. Both Christiano and Sylvia are trying far too hard to sound passionate with gasps and grunts and groans.

But Tom loves it and gives them a thumbs up.

EXT. VENICE - PROMENADE - DAY

Christiano steps forward at the end of a song. He is taken aback by all the money in the violin case.

> CHRISTIANO: Look at this! You do this well every day and I'm taking lessons from you.

EXT. VENICE - BEACH - DAY

Casanova and Christiano walk along the beach, eating hot dogs. Casanova still has trouble keeping his eyes off the near-bare female bodies everywhere, but he looks more shocked than seduced by them.

> CHRISTIANO: I got a lead on a dude named Larry the Eye who may be able to help us. He's into all kinds of magic. I'm trying to track down the particulars. Meanwhile I think I talked Tom into giving you a spot in the movie – I thought you'd need the money, but it looks like you're doing better than me. I told him we'd stop by tonight and talk about it.

He notices that Casanova's attention has been elsewhere.

> CHRISTIANO: Tom knows a lot of girls if you're horny.

Casanova shoots him a puzzling look and Christiano gives him the gesture of sexual intercourse, the index finger of one hand going in and out of a circle formed by the thumb and index finger of the other.

> CASANOVA: What has this place done to you? You act like one of them!
>
> CHRISTIANO: What did I do?
>
> CASANOVA: Everything here is so ... literal! So obvious! There is no mystery. Where is the temptation and the danger and the anticipation and the seduction? The teasing flash of white flesh under parting silk? A woman's most sensual gesture is her modesty – but no one here is modest. The women here sweat like farm hands – and are twice as brown!

He storms off, leaving Christiano stunned.

> CHRISTIANO: *(after him)* Give it a few weeks! You'll end up loving it here! I'm even thinking of staying!

INT. TOM SNOW PRODUCTIONS - OFFICE - NIGHT

Tom is watching dailies when Christiano enters.

> TOM: You're late. Where's your cousin?
>
> CHRISTIANO: I don't know.
>
> TOM: Goddamn it, I already had a writer come up with a scene for him. I want to shoot it first thing in the morning.

CHRISTIANO: I'll tell him. How are the dailies?

TOM: Terrible. I said groan with passion. You sound like you're stuck in the middle of a shit.

INT. TOM SNOW PRODUCTIONS - BASEMENT - DAY

Casanova is tuning the violin.

CHRISTIANO: I promised Tom you'd be here when he comes in this morning.

CASANOVA: I will not be in your movie.

CHRISTIANO: I think it's just a screen test. It won't take long.

Casanova goes about his business.

CHRISTIANO: Do it for me. Because without me, where would you be now? And who's going to find the magic that will get us home again?

CASANOVA: For you, I will stay for this screen test. But I will not be in your movie.

EXT. TOM SNOW PRODUCTIONS - BACK ENTRANCE - DAY

A van is backing up against an open door, where

several WORKERS wait.

Along a nearby fence picketers are hollering.

> PICKETER #1: Pornography is rape!
>
> PICKETER #2: Pornography demeans women!

Tom gets out and gives the picketers the finger. This only makes them holler more.

> TOM: *(to the workers)* Bring it down the stairs to the basement.

He enters the building.

The workers open the back door of the van. Inside is a strange looking piece of equipment, suggesting an exercise machine.

> WORKER #1: What the hell's he doing, going on an exercise program?
>
> WORKER #2: Look there – handcuffs. It's some kind of torture machine.

INT. TOM SNOW PRODUCTIONS - BASEMENT - DAY

MARIGOLD, young and buxom, fully-clothed, is demonstrating the piece of equipment. She is stretched out on her back, spread-eagled with both her feet and hands cuffed to parts of the machinery.

Tom stands next to her. Watching are Casanova and Christiano.

>TOM: Amado, come over here.

Casanova steps forward.

>TOM: Here's the sequence. First you straddle her, she sucks your cock for a while. Then you take this here ...

He pulls a long dildo from the equipment.

>TOM: ... use it vaginally, use it anally, then you make her suck it, then both it and your cock together. Can you remember that?

Casanova looks like a volcano about to explode.

>MARIGOLD: It's a piece of cake, sugar, believe me.

>CASANOVA: We are not animals!

>TOM: *(to Christiano)* Is he serious?

>CASANOVA: A man and woman together do not need machinery!

He makes for the stairs.

>MARIGOLD: Tom, where'd you find this guy?

>TOM: *(after him)* Hey, I already paid a

writer fifty bucks for this scene!

CHRISTIANO: He hasn't really adjusted from the old country yet.

TOM: Fuck. This is a great scene. *(to Christiano)* You're gonna have to do it yourself.

CHRISTIANO: I will make the sacrifice for art.

MARIGOLD: Hoop-dee doo!

EXT. TOM SNOW PRODUCTIONS - DAY

Casanova comes out the back door. Seeing him, the picketers get noisy again.

Casanova walks over to the chain-link fence. A picketer rushes forward and spits in his face.

PICKETER #1: Pornography degrades women!

Casanova wipes himself off.

PICKETER #2: Pornography rapes the human soul!

CASANOVA: That is very well put.

PICKETER #3: Pornography–

PICKETER #1: Wait a minute! What did you

say?

CASANOVA: I agree with you.

PICKETER #1: You do?

CASANOVA: Do you know what they do down there? It is the most disgusting thing I have ever seen.

Picketer #2, whose name is SHARON, comes forward.

SHARON: My brother writes for the weekly. Would you let him interview you?

INT. WEEKLY PAPER - OFFICE - DAY

Casanova sits in a chair while a PHOTOGRAPHER snaps photos. Sitting next to him is Sharon.

VIC, her brother the reporter, rushes in and plops down behind the desk.

VIC: Sorry I'm late. You got what you need?

PHOTOGRAPHER: Got it.

He leaves.

VIC: On the phone, Sharon said you're an employee at Tom Snow Productions and will go on record about the movies they make. True?

CASANOVA: Yes, I know what happens in the basement.

VIC: All right! First your name ... spell it ...

He grabs a pad and pen.

CASANOVA: Giacomo Casanova. G-I-A–

VIC: Wait a minute. What's the deal here?

CASANOVA: You wanted me to spell my name.

VIC: Your real name.

CASANOVA: Giacomo Girolamo Casanova.

VIC: You're pulling my leg.

CASANOVA: My name is my name. I was born in Venice, Italy, on April 2, 1725 and–

Vic throws down the pen and stands up.

VIC: Sharon, get him the hell out of here. This is the last time I'm letting you do this to me!

EXT. VENICE - PROMENADE - DAY

Casanova and Sharon walk along together.

SHARON: Why did you have to carry on like that?

CASANOVA: I told him the truth.

Someone hands Casanova a flier. It reads: "Past Life Regression. Learn about your past lives. Classes taught by a metaphysical minister."

Casanova folds up the flier and saves it.

SHARON: If you were really Casanova, then you wouldn't have said the things you did because Casanova was as bad as the rest of them. No, he was one of the worst. He used women as objects.

CASANOVA: That is not true!

SHARON: The greatest seducer of all time! The big stud of the ages! Give me a break.

CASANOVA: Who told you this?

SHARON: It's common knowledge.

CASANOVA: Where would I find out about this?

SHARON: Ask anyone. Go to the library.

EXT. VENICE - LIBRARY - DAY

Casanova walks into the library.

INT. VENICE - LIBRARY - DAY

He enters cautiously and looks around. He sees an Information Desk and goes to it.

INT. VENICE - LIBRARY - REFERENCE ROOM - DAY

Casanova sits at a table, reading an encyclopedia entry about Casanova. What he's reading is making him very upset.

Finally he slams the book shut in disgust. He stands up.

> CASANOVA: This book is filled with lies!

Other PEOPLE nearby look at him in shock.

EXT. VENICE - LIBRARY - DAY

Casanova races out of the library. He looks like a man on a mission.

INT. TOM SNOW PRODUCTIONS - FRONT DESK - DAY

Casanova comes in, going quickly to the staircase to the basement. He passes by before Sylvia can say anything.

INT. TOM SNOW PRODUCTIONS - OFFICE - DAY

Tom is at his desk when Casanova flees past the doorway.

TOM: Hey! I want to talk to you!

INT. TOM SNOW PRODUCTIONS - BASEMENT - DAY

Casanova races down the stairs.

Christiano is going over lines.

> CHRISTIANO: You got me in deep shit.

Tom comes down the stairs.

> TOM: Hey!

Casanova rolls up his sleeping bag. He takes the shopping bag with his native clothes and dumps them on the mattress.

> TOM: I do you a favor, I expect one in return.
>
> CHRISTIANO: Let me handle it. He's obviously upset about something.
>
> TOM: *(to Casanova)* I didn't have to give you an opportunity here.
>
> CHRISTIANO: Tom, let me find out what's going on.
>
> TOM: I expect a full report!

He climbs the stairs.

Casanova is changing clothes, getting back into the frills of the 18th century.

> CHRISTIANO: What the hell do you think you're doing?
>
> CASANOVA: History has decided that I rape women. I manipulate them for my own selfish pleasure. What books say about me, I would be no better than an animal, or the people in this movie of yours. History does not know the first thing about me!
>
> CHRISTIANO: So you think you can change history? Lots of luck.
>
> CASANOVA: I can be who I am until I figure out how to escape this insane asylum!

He picks up the violin, grabs the sleeping bag and heads for the stairs.

> CHRISTIANO: Where do you expect to stay?
>
> CASANOVA: On the sand! There is plenty to go around.
>
> CHRISTIANO: I'm seeing Larry the Eye tonight. This could be our big break.

But it goes on deaf ears.

> CHRISTIANO: *(after him)* I need to know how to find you!

EXT. VENICE - BEACH - DAY

Casanova, violin in one hand, sleeping bag in the other, plods along the beach.

EXT. VENICE - BEACH - DAY - LATER

He continues walking along the beach. Far less people are around as he moves away from town and the Promenade.

EXT. COAST - SECLUDED BEACH - DAY

He finally reaches a secluded area of beach. He drops to the sand, exhausted.

EXT. COAST - SECLUDED BEACH - NIGHT

Casanova sits around a campfire on the beach, playing his violin.

The sky is filled with stars. The ocean waves lap against the sand. His music flows over the scene like a delicate breeze.

EXT. COAST - SECLUDED BEACH - DAY

Early morning. A security patrol jeep stops next to where Casanova is sleeping on the sand.

A SECURITY OFFICER gets out and nudges Casanova with his foot.

Casanova stirs.

> SECURITY OFFICER: You can't sleep on the beach.
>
> CASANOVA: Go away.

Casanova closes his eyes.

The security officer goes to the jeep and picks up the intercom.

> SECURITY OFFICER: Gonna need a van here.

EXT. VENICE - POLICE STATION - DAY

The jeep and a police van are parked in front of a small building, the police station.

INT. VENICE - POLICE STATION - DAY

The security officer signs a paper at a front desk.

> SECURITY OFFICER: He's all yours.

INT. VENICE - POLICE STATION - ROOM - DAY

Casanova sits at a table. LT. MASTERS comes in, carrying a clipboard.

> LT. MASTERS: You've been arrested for sleeping on the beach and vagrancy. Do you understand that?

CASANOVA: No.

LT. MASTERS: What part of it don't you understand?

CASANOVA: Why is it against the law to go to sleep?

LT. MASTERS: It says here you gave your name as Casanova. What's your real name?

CASANOVA: Giacomo Casanova. I was born in Venice, Italy, on April 2, 1725.

Lt. Masters shakes his head and leaves.

EXT. HENNY'S OFFICE - DAY

A police van is parked outside. BRUCE, the van driver, is smoking a cigarette.

BETTY SUE, Henny's secretary, comes outside and quickly lights up.

BRUCE: Hi, Betty Sue.

BETTY SUE: Hi, Bruce. Looks like you brought us a real live one today.

BRUCE: Flashiest dresser since I brought you Mae West.

INT. HENNY'S OFFICE - DAY

Casanova, in his frills, sits across the desk from

Henny.

> HENNY: Amado, I just don't understand what happened to you. I've been trying to get ahold of Chris. My first job is to determine whether it's safe to let you back out on the street.

A silence.

> HENNY: Clamming up isn't going to help you.
>
> CASANOVA: You keep calling me Amado. Address me by my name and I will talk to you.
>
> HENNY: I really can't make a decision until I talk to Chris.
>
> CASANOVA: Christiano is looking for the magic to take us home.
>
> HENNY: <u>Us</u> home? He dropped through this worm hole with you?
>
> CASANOVA: I know nothing about a worm hole. He was given the magic potion first.
>
> HENNY: Interesting. Okay, I have what I need. You can go.

She stops him at the door.

> HENNY: It's a shame, Amado. When I first

met you, you were very charming.

EXT. HENNY'S OFFICE - DAY

Bruce and Betty Sue are making out when Casanova comes outside. They quickly separate, and Bruce leads Casanova into the secure back of the van.

INT. VENICE - POLICE STATION - FRONT DESK - DAY

Bruce brings Casanova in.

> CASANOVA: I want to leave now.
>
> FRONT DESK OFFICER: Just hold it a sec.

Bruce hands him a clipboard. He quickly reads over it.

> FRONT DESK OFFICER: Sorry, Casanova. The doc didn't approve your release.

INT. VENICE - POLICE STATION - CELL - DAY

Casanova sits alone in a cell.

EXT. TOM SNOW PRODUCTIONS - NIGHT

A couple of cars are parked out front.

INT. TOM SNOW PRODUCTIONS - OFFICE - NIGHT

Tom is hosting a party for a few other porno filmmakers. They are watching a video of dailies of the scene on the mechanical contraption.

> TOM: Is that hot or what? I'm gonna do one about a robot dating service. Sex machines are gonna be the new rage.

In a corner of the office is Christiano, on the phone. He hangs up.

> CHRISTIANO: Tom, my cousin's in jail. I gotta see if I can get him out.

> TOM: Let him rot in there! *(to the others)* Asshole thought he was too good to be in my movie.

EXT. VENICE - UPSCALE NEIGHBORHOOD /CANAL - NIGHT

Christiano walks along a canal in an upscale neighborhood.

INT. HENNY'S HOUSE - DINING ROOM - NIGHT

Henny and Ted are having after-dinner wine when the doorbell rings.

Henny goes to the door.

INT. HENNY'S HOUSE - ENTRANCE - NIGHT

Henny finds Christiano at the door.

> CHRISTIANO: Sorry to disturb you at home but it's urgent. Amado's in jail. He can't get out on bail unless you sign a paper.
>
> HENNY: I'm not sure I can. He won't give up his delusions.
>
> CHRISTIANO: He fell on his head as a kid. He gets these relapses but they always go away.

Henny studies him carefully.

> CHRISTIANO: This trip was supposed to be therapy for him. Give him a change of scenery, maybe things would get better. Guess they got worse.
>
> HENNY: A familiar environment is very important to keep some people stable.
>
> CHRISTIANO: I'm the only relative he's got around here.
>
> HENNY: I suppose I do owe him a favor. Come by my office first thing in the morning and we'll talk more.

TV SCREEN

Soft porn on a cable channel. A man's face in ecstasy, apparently getting a blow job.

INT. HENNY'S HOUSE - LIVING ROOM - NIGHT

Ted sits on the divan, watching the soft porn. Henny comes into the room.

> HENNY: I wish you'd ask before you turn on pay-per-view.
>
> TED: Do I look like that?
>
> HENNY: I hope not.

She heads off.

> TED: Where are you going?
>
> HENNY: To take a bath.

He lets her go and gets back to the soft porn.

EXT. VENICE - POLICE STATION - DAY

Casanova and Christiano come out of the station.

> CHRISTIANO: We have to have a serious talk.

EXT. CUPID'S RETREAT - PATIO - DAY

They sit at a small table.

> CHRISTIANO: Larry the Eye wants to meet you. He says the magic is personal, it depends on how the vibrations happen

between you. I made you an appointment. This guy's a night owl, so I had to make it late at night, tomorrow. Here's the address.

He hands Casanova a slip of paper.

> CASANOVA: The sooner, the better.
>
> CHRISTIANO: The thing is, I'm having second thoughts about going back.
>
> CASANOVA: You want to stay here?
>
> CHRISTIANO: It won't effect you going back one way or the other. I already asked.
>
> CASANOVA: How can you stand the vulgarity of this place?
>
> CHRISTIANO: It grows on you. And where else can I be a movie star?

INT. HENNY'S OFFICE - DAY

Henny gathers her things, getting ready to leave for the day.

Betty Sue appears in the doorway. Behind her is Casanova.

> BETTY SUE: He won't take no for an answer.
>
> HENNY: That's okay. Come in, Amado. Betty Sue, please shut the door.

Henny and Casanova are alone.

> CASANOVA: I want to thank you for signing the paper.
>
> HENNY: Don't make me regret it.
>
> CASANOVA: I am having a very hard time adjusting here.
>
> HENNY: You want to tell me about it?
>
> CASANOVA: Why is there so much ... I'm not sure I can explain it ...
>
> HENNY: So much ... ?
>
> CASANOVA: Skin.
>
> HENNY: Skin?
>
> CASANOVA: Exposure of skin. Everyone behaves as if the world is one big public spa, all the time. Everyone wants burned skin. Everyone is sweating all the time. Where I come from– ... I'm sorry, for a minute I thought you believed me. I should just say thank you and leave.

He turns to go.

> HENNY: Do you need a ride?

EXT. VENICE - STREET - DAY

Henny's car moves down a Venice street in the business area.

INT. HENNY'S CAR - DAY

Henny turns to Casanova.

> HENNY: Has Chris shown you any of the sights?
>
> CASANOVA: What sights?
>
> HENNY: I'll show you. Do you have time?
>
> CASANOVA: For you? Of course.

A SERIES OF SHOTS

of Henny giving Casanova the grand tour of the coast.

--They look at the yachts docked at a marina.

--They watch fishermen on the Santa Monica pier.

--They pose for a sidewalk portrait together.

--Henny tries to teach Casanova how to rollerskate along a beach path.

--They hike in the hills above Malibu.

EXT. COASTLINE - CLIFF - DAY

Casanova and Henny stand at a scenic view overlooking the ocean at Malibu. The sun is beginning to drop below the horizon.

Casanova recites a poem. As he continues, Henny becomes more and more the focus of his words, so that by poem's end they are standing close and looking into one another's eyes.

> CASANOVA: If questioning would make us wise, / No eyes would ever gaze in eyes; / If all our tale were told in speech, / No mouths would wander each to each. // Were spirits free from mortal mesh / And love not bound in hearts of flesh, / No aching breasts would yearn to meet / And find their ecstasy complete. //

They face one another.

> CASANOVA: For who is there that lives and knows / The secret powers by which he grows? / Were knowledge all, what were our need / To thrill and faint and sweetly bleed? // Then seek not, sweet, the "If" and "Why"; / I love you now until I die. / For I must love because I live / And life in me is what you give.

They stand closer than ever.

> HENNY: That's so beautiful ... did you write it?

CASANOVA: Unfortunately, I do not write that well. It popped into my head. Like magic.

HENNY: My training is scientific. That makes me very skeptical about magic.

CASANOVA: When I was a child, I had chronic nose bleeds all the time. The doctors had no idea what to do. Everyone assumed I would eventually bleed to death. Then my mother took me to an old woman who practiced magic. She put me in a seaman's trunk and covered me with magic herbs, then closed the lid. When I was allowed to come back out, I never had a nose bleed again.

HENNY: That's child abuse. How long were you in there?

CASANOVA: Long enough. I was cured. But my mother abandoned me anyway. She was an actress and I was too much bother.

HENNY: Interesting. Who raised you?

CASANOVA: My grandmother – until a nobleman, Matteo Bragadin, took me under his wing. He treated me like a son.

Their lips almost touch. Henny closes her eyes. Casanova bends forward enough to kiss her.

A long, gentle kiss. Then they exchange a deep look.

Henny is flustered. She starts to say something but Casanova puts a finger on her lips.

> CASANOVA: "If all our tale were told in speech, / No mouths would wander each to each."

But Henny won't be kissed again. She steps back.

> HENNY: I'd better take you home.

EXT. COAST HIGHWAY - NIGHT

She drives along the coast after sunset.

INT. HENNY'S CAR - NIGHT

Casanova has been staring at her.

> HENNY: You make me nervous.

> CASANOVA: Why are you so afraid of love?

> HENNY: I beg your pardon. I'm engaged to be married.

> CASANOVA: You felt something special when we kissed.

> HENNY: I don't want to talk about it.

> CASANOVA: Did I say I wanted to talk? I want to love.

HENNY: Just take me to bed like that, huh? Maybe you really are Casanova.

CASANOVA: I would never do that! It is much too early. We would miss so many wonderful steps along the way. The journey should be as pleasurable as the destination.

HENNY: You're a funny one, Amado Casanova whoever you are.

EXT. TOM SNOW PRODUCTIONS - NIGHT

Henny's car stops in front of the studio.

INT. HENNY'S CAR - NIGHT

She waits for him to get out.

HENNY: Aren't you getting out?

CASANOVA: I stopped staying here.

HENNY: Where are you staying?

CASANOVA: On the beach. But for some reason, this is not allowed.

HENNY: I see. So what do we do now?

CASANOVA: This is not your problem.

He opens the door and gets out.

EXT. TOM SNOW PRODUCTIONS - NIGHT

Casanova starts walking away. The car doesn't move.

INT. HENNY'S CAR - NIGHT

She doesn't know what to do. Finally she drives up beside him.

INT./EXT. HENNY'S CAR - NIGHT

> HENNY: If you sleep on the beach, you'll be arrested again. I can't help you a second time.
>
> CASANOVA: Stop worrying about it.

He keeps walking, she keeps creeping along beside him.

> HENNY: Get in.
>
> CASANOVA: I'll be fine.
>
> HENNY: You can sleep on the couch. Only tonight!

He keeps walking.

> HENNY: Goddamn it, get in!

Casanova stops and smiles. He gets in.

EXT. VENICE - UPSCALE NEIGHBORHOOD /CANAL - HENNY'S HOUSE - NIGHT

Henny parks and they get out. Casanova admires the canal passing by.

>HENNY: Originally Venice was designed to be like your home. Most of the canals got destroyed years ago. It's still beautiful, isn't it?

>CASANOVA: I would like to take you to Italy.

INT. HENNY'S HOUSE - LIVING ROOM - NIGHT

Henny tosses a pile of sheets on the divan.

>HENNY: You have to make your own bed.

>CASANOVA: And lie in it, too.

>HENNY: Goodnight.

>CASANOVA: May you have sweet dreams.

>HENNY: Of you, right?

>CASANOVA: That is up to you.

He smiles. She leaves.

INT. HENNY'S HOUSE - NIGHT - LATER

Late, dark. Casanova sleeps on the divan.

The door cracks open. A figure creeps in.

Casanova opens his eyes, listening. The figure moves slowly across the carpet next to him.

The figure moves into the hallway. Casanova slips out of bed and tip-toes after him.

INT. HENNY'S HOUSE - BEDROOM - NIGHT

The figure enters Henny's bedroom.

Suddenly Casanova leaps through the doorway, jumping him. Both fall on the foot of Henny's bed.

Henny wakes and turns on the bedside lamp.

Wrestling at the foot of the bed are Casanova – and Ted.

> HENNY: Ted! Amado, stop it, it's Ted!

Casanova has a grip on him.

> HENNY: Amado, stop it! Casanova!

She looks around for something to use as a weapon. All she can find is her briefcase. She picks it up and raises it over her head, looking a little ridiculous.

> HENNY: Stop it!

Seeing her, Casanova releases his grip. He stands up.

Ted brushes himself off and picks up a bouquet of flowers off the floor.

> HENNY: What the hell are you doing here?
>
> TED: I can see you weren't expecting me.
>
> HENNY: Amado, leave us alone, please.
>
> CASANOVA: Casanova.

He bows, turns and leaves.

> TED: Casanova?
>
> HENNY: It's a long story.
>
> TED: What the hell's he doing here?
>
> HENNY: I asked you first.
>
> TED: I thought I'd surprise you. Make up for our little spat.

He holds out the bouquet for her.

> HENNY: I don't believe this.

INT. HENNY'S HOUSE - KITCHEN - NIGHT

Henny is putting the flowers in a vase. Casanova and Ted sit at a table.

HENNY: I'm helping him get settled at the shelter.

TED: What's that got to do with me spending the night?

HENNY: Because I don't want you here tonight. It's just not a good time.

TED: I see.

He stands up.

HENNY: Quit acting like you're jealous.

TED: Of Casanova? Don Juan, I'd have trouble with.

Ted heads for the door. Henny puts down what she's doing and chases him.

INT. HENNY'S HOUSE - ENTRANCE - NIGHT

She catches him at the door.

HENNY: It was a sweet thought.

TED: But timing is everything.

HENNY: Quit trying to make me feel guilty. I haven't done anything wrong here.

INT. HENNY'S HOUSE - KITCHEN - NIGHT

Henny returns and finishes arranging the flowers.

> HENNY: I'm going back to bed.

Before she is gone, she stops and turns.

> HENNY: Thank you. It was a courageous thing for you to do, actually.
>
> CASANOVA: I had no time to think about it.

INT. HENNY'S HOUSE - LIVING ROOM - NIGHT

Casanova gets back into bed.

INT. HENNY'S HOUSE - BEDROOM - NIGHT

Henny gets into bed and turns out the light.

INT. HENNY'S HOUSE - LIVING ROOM - NIGHT

Casanova closes his eyes. He hears a voice in his head.

> CASANOVA: *(V.O.)* "If questioning would make us wise, / No eyes would ever gaze in eyes."

INT. HENNY'S HOUSE - BEDROOM - NIGHT

Henny hears Casanova's voice in her head.

> HENNY: *(V.O.)* "If all our tale were told in speech, / No mouths would wander each to each."

She sighs and rolls over.

EXT. VENICE - SHELTER - DAY

Casanova is in line with other homeless people in front of a storefront. He carries the violin and the sleeping bag. He's still in his frills but nobody pays this any mind.

Henny comes out of the building.

> HENNY: Okay, you're all set. You'll have to fill out a registration card.

She leans close to speak softly.

> HENNY: Don't say you were born in the 18th century. Use 1977, that's about right.

She suddenly looks at him differently.

> CASANOVA: Why are you looking at me like that?

> HENNY: You're so young.

CASANOVA: My soul is immortal.

She starts away. He grabs her hand.

CASANOVA: When will I see you again?

HENNY: I don't know.

CASANOVA: Dinner tonight.

HENNY: I'll have to think about it.

CASANOVA: Come to Cupid's Retreat at six.

HENNY: I'm not promising anything.

She pulls free. As she goes, she looks back to find him smiling at her. She can't help herself – and smiles back.

In line, Casanova notices that everyone is looking at him. He bows theatrically.

INT. SHELTER - DAY

Casanova reaches a table and is given a registration form to fill out.

SHELTER CLERK: Fill as much of this out as you can. Curfew is nine p.m.

CASANOVA: I don't understand.

SHELTER CLERK: After nine, the doors are locked. At 8:45, vacant reserved cots are given out on a first come, first served basis.

CASANOVA: But I'm meeting Larry the Eye at ten.

SHELTER CLERK: Curfew is nine, sir.

Casanova moves out of line, and the next person steps up.

EXT. VENICE - PROMENADE - DAY

Casanova gets ready to play his violin.

The owner of the adjacent store is sweeping outside.

Nearby the sword swallower is back and doing his routine to a small crowd.

Casanova starts playing a melancholy piece. People gather. The business owner stops sweeping to listen. The sword swallower sees his audience disperse to gather near Casanova.

Casanova keeps playing, the music sad and haunting. People drop bills into the open violin case.

The sword swallower appears in the crowd. He maneuvers his way to the open violin case. He drops in a one-dollar bill, then takes a large handful of bills back.

Casanova catches him doing this. The sword

swallower turns to go, and Casanova stops playing.

> CASANOVA: Put the money back!

The sword swallower turns and grins.

> SWORD SWALLOWER: You're new here. We share all of our proceeds. It's a community togetherness thing.

> CASANOVA: Put it back!

Casanova points the violin bow at him, a threat.

The sword swallower grins and draws his sword.

> SWORD SWALLOWER: Are you sure you know what you're getting into?

> CASANOVA: You have no right to take my money.

> SWORD SWALLOWER: Consider it paying your dues.

Casanova makes a thrust with the violin bow. The sword swallower counters with a thrust of his sword.

Casanova realizes his disadvantage and backs up as the sword swallower advances with amateurish thrusts. Casanova easily dodges the sword but has no weapon for offense.

The nearby store owner holds up his broom.

STORE OWNER: Music man! Use this!

He tosses the broom, and Casanova one-hands it. He drops the violin bow and uses the broom like a sword.

Now they fight in earnest, though the sword swallower is no match for Casanova, a skilled swordsman. The sword swallower retreats until he is trapped against a doorway.

With one powerful thrust, Casanova knocks the sword to the ground.

> SWORD SWALLOWER: Okay, you win! You don't want to be a community person, fine. I'll give you your money back.
>
> CASANOVA: Yes, you will.

The sword swallower holds out the bills he took. Casanova grabs them. Quickly the sword swallower picks up his sword and disappears into the crowd.

Suddenly the crowd applauds. Casanova is surprised but then recovers, grins, and bows.

EXT. HENNY'S OFFICE - DAY

Ted's convertible skids to a stop outside, almost running into the building.

INT. HENNY'S OFFICE - DAY

Ted storms inside past Betty Sue's desk and into Henny's office.

Henny is on the phone.

>TED: I don't fucking believe you.

>HENNY: I'm on the phone.

He reaches forward and hangs her up.

>TED: Breaking our engagement on voice mail! You're supposed to be a psychiatrist and have better communication skills than that!

>HENNY: And you're supposed to be a lawyer and know about diplomacy! You're behaving just the way I feared you would.

>TED: That Casanova lunatic has something to do with this, doesn't he?

>HENNY: He made me realize I'm not ready to get married again. I still want to see you, but–

>TED: We'd set the date. The invitations are at the printer.

>HENNY: That's just money. I'm talking about my life. I have to know I'm ready.

>TED: Well, great. If you ever decide, you've got my number.

HENNY: Why can't we go on like before?

TED: Because you've changed, that's why!

He bolts out of there.

Betty Sue appears in the office doorway.

BETTY SUE: Are you okay?

HENNY: I know it doesn't look like it, but I think I'm really pretty good here.

EXT. CUPID'S RETREAT - PATIO - DAY

Casanova sits alone at a table, waiting. His sleeping bag and violin are on a chair.

EXT. CUPID'S RETREAT - DAY

Across the Promenade, Henny paces back and forth. Should she or shouldn't she?

EXT. CUPID'S RETREAT - PATIO - DAY

Casanova stands up. He picks up his stuff.

EXT. CUPID'S RETREAT - DAY

Henny still hasn't made up her mind when Casanova comes out. She turns her back to him, retreating into a doorway.

She watches him head down the Promenade. She

looks like she made a mistake.

EXT. VENICE - PROMENADE - DAY

Someone shoves a flier at Casanova. It reads: "Is Your Inner Child Gay?"

Casanova crumples it and throws it back.

EXT. VENICE - POOR NEIGHBORHOOD - NIGHT

Casanova looks for the address Christiano gave him. He's getting close.

EXT. POOR NEIGHBORHOOD - HOUSE - NIGHT

He finds the address, a run-down house from which loud rock music blares.

Casanova steps up onto the porch. He rings the doorbell. Nothing. He knocks as loud as he can. Nothing.

The music blares out but inside there is only candlelight.

Casanova sees that the front door is cracked open.

INT. POOR NEIGHBORHOOD - HOUSE - NIGHT

Casanova comes inside.

CASANOVA: Hello?

Candles are everywhere, the only illumination. Suddenly the music stops.

CASANOVA: Hello?

VOICE: *(O.S.)* In the kitchen!

INT. HOUSE - KITCHEN - NIGHT

Casanova enters the kitchen. At the stove is a giant of a man, LARRY THE EYE, 50s, bald, graying beard. His name comes from a patch over one eye, which gives the visible eye great intensity.

He is stirring something in a large pot on the stove.

CASANOVA: Christiano made an appointment for me. I assume you are ... *(looking at slip of paper)* ... Larry the Eye?

LARRY THE EYE: I've been expecting you. Stand still a minute.

Casanova obeys.

LARRY THE EYE: Good vibes, good vibes. Sit down, I won't be a sec.

Casanova takes a seat at a small table.

LARRY THE EYE: I'm going to be upfront with you. Time travel ain't exactly my deal. But I've read about it, I'm willing to try it.

> Since I can't guarantee the results, I'll only charge half my usual price. Two-hundred and fifty dollars, payable in advance.
>
> CASANOVA: It will take me a few weeks to save that much.
>
> LARRY THE EYE: No hurry. Meanwhile, I'm going to need something from the time and place of your destination.
>
> CASANOVA: A piece of my clothing? A coin?
>
> LARRY THE EYE: If it's from where you want to go, it's perfect.

He steps away from the stove and approaches Casanova. He takes out a switchblade and snaps it open. Before Casanova can react, he's grabbed his hair and cut off a piece.

> LARRY THE EYE: And a hair sample. You got money you can put down to get me started?

EXT. POOR NEIGHBORHOOD - HOUSE - NIGHT

Larry the Eye walks Casanova outside.

> LARRY THE EYE: I don't know why but I thought you wanted to go back to the Middle Ages or something. 1749 shouldn't be too difficult.

CASANOVA: And if this does not work?

LARRY THE EYE: Well, I've found three different formulas, and I'm still doing research. We can keep trying.

EXT. POOR NEIGHBORHOOD - STREET - NIGHT

Casanova is walking on a dark street when TWO HOODLUMS come out of the shadows. They jump him, knocking him to the ground.

Casanova takes both of them on. He's holding his own.

He gets tripped to the ground, and one of the hoodlums runs off with the violin and sleeping bag.

The other hoodlum jumps at Casanova, who rolls out of the way. He scurries on top of the hoodlum, then knocks him cold.

Casanova slowly gets to his feet. He nudges the hoodlum on the ground. Nothing.

He touches his own nose, which is bleeding.

A SERIES OF SHOTS (MEMORY FLASH)

of Casanova as a child with nose bleeds.

A nose bleed in a park.

A nose bleed at his grandmother's.

A nose bleed at home in bed.

INT. HENNY'S HOUSE - NIGHT - (PRESENT)

Henny, in her robe, responds to a knock on the door. She looks through the peep hole and gasps. She opens the door.

The blood at Casanova's nose has dried and one eye is bruised.

> HENNY: My God, what happened?

INT. HENNY'S HOUSE - KITCHEN - NIGHT

Henny is tending to Casanova's wounds.

He looks up at her. Their eyes meet. She bends down and kisses him.

INT. HENNY'S HOUSE - LIVING ROOM - NIGHT

Casanova goes to the divan.

> CASANOVA: May I have sheets?
>
> HENNY: You don't have to sleep on the couch unless you want to.

He looks at her, studying her meaning.

CASANOVA: Are you seducing me?

HENNY: Yes, I guess I am. Does it bother you?

CASANOVA: I think it does. We still have much to learn about one another.

HENNY: But you're Casanova, I thought you'd turned seduction into an art form.

CASANOVA: You are mocking me.

HENNY: I'm sorry. I only meant that Casanova was always taking women to bed.

CASANOVA: Only if they wanted to, and only after courting them.

HENNY: Fine. Back to the point. I'm inviting you to come to bed with me.

CASANOVA: Why?

HENNY: Why? Because I find you attractive and I want to explore my feelings for you.

CASANOVA: You can still do that if I spend the night right here.

HENNY: You're a funny one. Most men would jump at the opportunity.

CASANOVA: I am not most men.

> HENNY: It's hard to believe Casanova, the great over, would turn me down.
>
> CASANOVA: Because you really know nothing about me. What I read in the library, this is no one I recognize. I have never taken a woman against her will in my life.
>
> HENNY: This is not against my will, Amado.
>
> CASANOVA: See? You still refuse to believe me.
>
> HENNY: Shit. Is that what this is about? Me going along with you? Fine. I'll call you whatever you like.

He moves for the door.

> HENNY: Where are you going?
>
> CASANOVA: I can sleep on the beach.
>
> HENNY: You'll be arrested again.

He doesn't reply and leaves her upset.

EXT. TOM SNOW PRODUCTIONS - NIGHT

Casanova goes to the back of the building. He snuggles as best he can into the doorway.

EXT. TOM SNOW PRODUCTIONS - DAY

The back door opens, jarring Casanova awake. Christiano comes outside.

> CHRISTIANO: What happened to you?
>
> CASANOVA: I got robbed.
>
> CHRISTIANO: Did you see Larry the Eye?
>
> CASANOVA: I need to give him some money, but they took my violin.
>
> CHRISTIANO: Shit. I don't know if I can get another one or not. Come on, I'll buy you coffee.

EXT. VENICE - BEACH - DAY

They wade in the waves, carrying styrofoam coffee cups.

> CHRISTIANO: I can loan you maybe half.
>
> CASANOVA: You need it for yourself.
>
> CHRISTIANO: You'll be going back first. I want to make sure the magic doesn't kill you. Just kidding. I promised Tom I'd do another movie after this one. He's got a sequel, "Casanova Does Casablanca." He wants me to play Bogart.
>
> CASANOVA: You are like a stranger to me.
>
> CHRISTIANO: Should've seen me six

months ago, I was like you, in total shock.

CASANOVA: This place will always shock me.

CHRISTIANO: You get used to it. Life is so much easier here. I mean, look at this beach! Look at that ocean!

Spontaneously Christiano runs into the water, diving, swimming out. He shouts for joy.

Casanova watches a moment, then turns and goes.

EXT. VENICE - PROMENADE - DAY

Casanova turns down a flier thrust at him. He remembers the flier he saved and takes it out, unfolding it.

He reads it again: "Past Life Regression. Learn about your past lives. Classes taught by a metaphysical minister."

There's an address.

EXT. VENICE - CHURCH OF METAPHYSICAL TRUTH - DAY

Casanova finds the small church, which is located in a Spanish bungalow, a residence. A hand-painted sign over the porch reads "Church of Metaphysical Truth."

INT. VENICE - CHURCH OF META-

PHYSICAL TRUTH - DAY

Casanova comes into an entryway. Hearing him, REV. SUN comes out of an office. He wears a priest's collar, looks about 40.

> REV. SUN: May I help you?
>
> CASANOVA: I hope so. I have your flier about ...

He looks at the flier.

> CASANOVA: ... past life regression.
>
> REV. SUN: Our next class starts in August. I can give you a brochure.
>
> CASANOVA: I do not want a class. I want to go back to 1749 where I belong. To Venice, Italy. I thought maybe you could help me.

Rev. Sun studies him.

> REV. SUN: Come into my office.

INT. CHURCH OF METAPHYSICAL TRUTH - OFFICE - DAY

Casanova has told Rev. Sun his story.

> REV. SUN: Let me see if I understand you. You actually are not visiting a past life – but a future life. You've done past life regression in reverse. Future life premonition, I

suppose it's called.

> CASANOVA: I want to return where I belong. I found someone who can do the magic. The problem is, I have no money.

> REV. SUN: No money. I see.

He is thinking.

> REV. SUN: Well, then: how would you like to make some money?

EXT. SECLUDED BEACH - DAY

An old station wagon comes down a dirt road to a dilapidated cabin along a secluded beach. It parks, and Rev. Sun and Casanova get out.

> REV. SUN: It's not much but it's better than being a vagrant.

Casanova is impressed, especially with the view.

> REV. SUN: I haven't been here yet this season. Let's see what kind of shape it's in.

INT. SECLUDED BEACH - CABIN - DAY

They come inside. Lots of garbage, evidence of people having used the place.

Sunlight streams through openings in the roof. But it's livable.

Rev. Sun opens a cupboard.

> REV. SUN: They even left you some canned food. What do you think?
>
> CASANOVA: It is wonderful!
>
> REV. SUN: I'll be back in a day or two with more supplies. How's Chef Boyardee sound? I need to get publicity out right away. Think you can have your first lecture ready in two weeks?
>
> CASANOVA: Two weeks is fine.
>
> REV. SUN: Excellent. You have a question about anything?
>
> CASANOVA: How far is it to walk to town?
>
> REV. SUN: The nearest community of any size is Malibu. It's too far to walk, you'd have to hitch-hike.
>
> CASANOVA: Please tell me how to do this.

EXT. BEACH HIGHWAY - DAY

Casanova, still in 18th century frills, holds out his thumb. A car zooms by.

EXT. HIGHWAY - NEAR MALIBU - DAY

A car lets Casanova off. He holds out his thumb for another ride.

INT. HENNY'S OFFICE - FRONT DESK - DAY

Henny comes out of her office.

>HENNY: I'm leaving early today.

>BETTY SUE: Don't forget you have a nine o'clock tomorrow.

>HENNY: Damn. Cancel it. I'm taking a few days off.

She walks out before Betty Sue can respond.

EXT. HENNY'S OFFICE - DAY

Henny gets in her car and drives off.

As soon as she's gone, a car pulls in front of the office and lets Casanova off.

INT. HENNY'S OFFICE - FRONT DESK - DAY

Casanova enters.

>CASANOVA: I'm here to see Henny.

>BETTY SUE: She just went home for the day.

Casanova looks crestfallen.

> BETTY SUE: She said she's taking a few days off.
>
> CASANOVA: Thank you.

EXT. HENNY'S OFFICE - DAY

Casanova sticks out his thumb again.

INT. HENNY'S HOUSE - KITCHEN - DAY

Henny is opening a bottle of wine when the doorbell rings. She's changed into comfortable clothes.

She opens the door to find Casanova.

> HENNY: Hi.
>
> CASANOVA: Are you busy?
>
> HENNY: No. I was just opening a bottle of wine. Join me?
>
> CASANOVA: We can take it to my new home.
>
> HENNY: Oh?
>
> CASANOVA: Wait till you see it!

EXT. SECLUDED BEACH - CABIN - DAY

Henny's car comes down the dirt road and stops.

She and Casanova get out.

> HENNY: How did you get this?

> CASANOVA: *(ignoring this)* Come on.

INT. SECLUDED BEACH - CABIN - DAY

They step inside. Henny can see blue sky through the gaps in the roof.

> HENNY: Very romantic. You're trespassing, aren't you?

> CASANOVA: I have a job. I get to use this while I prepare a lecture. I get half the gate receipts.

> HENNY: Slow down, you're losing me.

Casanova takes her hand.

> CASANOVA: I want to walk on the beach.

EXT. SECLUDED BEACH - DAY

They walk, holding hands, along the beach.

They stop, look at one another and kiss. Slow, deep.

> HENNY: You're getting me hot. I need a swim.

Keeping on her shorts and blouse, she runs into the water. Casanova chases her.

They swim and frolic. A water fight starts. They are like adolescents in love.

They stand close. Another kiss, slow and deep. Casanova kisses her neck.

> CASANOVA: Will you stay with me tonight?
>
> HENNY: You couldn't get rid of me.

INT. SECLUDED BEACH - CABIN - DAY

There is a mattress on the floor, some blankets heaped on top of them.

> HENNY: I don't know about your sleeping arrangements.

Casanova finds clean sheets in a closet.

> CASANOVA: Look!
>
> HENNY: A definite improvement.

They make the bed together, kissing now and then, flirting, teasing one another.

When they are done, Henny starts to undress.

> CASANOVA: No! Let me. You should be modest.

She stops, letting Casanova take over. He kisses her neck, moving his lips to the top button of her blouse.

He kisses the button, then undoes it. His lips move to the next button. He works slowly, teasingly, undoing each button as if it's a great pleasure and revelation in its own right.

The teasing slowness just gets Henny more excited.

> HENNY: Please ...

> CASANOVA: Everything in its time ...

He continues to undress her, step by slow step, teasing her unmercifully.

INT. SECLUDED BEACH - CABIN - DAY - LATER

Finally they are having intercourse. He looks deeply into her eyes and kisses her as his rhythm, and hers, increases to a passionate, mutual climax.

He collapses beside her. Both are breathing heavily.

> HENNY: My God ...

> CASANOVA: You saw Your God?

Henny chuckles.

> HENNY: Enough to make a believer out of me.

EXT. SECLUDED BEACH - CABIN - SUNSET

They sit close together, watching a spectacular sunset.

INT. SECLUDED BEACH - CABIN - NIGHT

They make love again.

Overhead, stars can be seen through the gaps in the roof.

EXT. SECLUDED BEACH - CABIN - DAY

The morning sun hits the cabin.

INT. SECLUDED BEACH - CABIN - DAY

Henny opens her eyes to find Casanova looking at her.

> HENNY: Good morning, sir.
>
> CASANOVA: Good morning.
>
> HENNY: I can't remember the last time I slept so well. This must be paradise.

EXT. SECLUDED BEACH - DAY

Casanova and Henny walk along the beach. Both wear shorts and tank tops.

They become playful, playing water tag in the waves.

INT. HENNY'S OFFICE - FRONT DESK - DAY

Ted comes in, carrying a large bouquet of flowers.

> TED: May I walk in and surprise her?
>
> BETTY SUE: She's not here. She took a few days off.
>
> TED: Really? Did she go somewhere?
>
> BETTY SUE: She didn't say.

EXT. HENNY'S HOUSE - PORCH - DAY

Ted stands at Henny's door with the flowers. He rings the doorbell again. No answer. He knocks. Nothing.

He gives up and leaves. Walking along the canal, he tosses the bouquet into the water.

EXT. SECLUDED BEACH - CABIN - DAY

Casanova and Henny are on a blanket, embraced and kissing.

Henny leaps up to her feet.

> HENNY: I feel so damn good! I'm going for a run. Want to come?
>
> CASANOVA: Running where?

HENNY: Down the beach.

CASANOVA: What for?

HENNY: To keep my heart healthy!

She jogs off. Casanova's expression reveals that he has no idea why she is suddenly running down the beach.

EXT. SECLUDED BEACH - CABIN - DAY - LATER

Casanova is dozing when the sound of a motor wakes him. He sits up to find the reverend's station wagon pulling up.

Rev. Sun gets out. He opens the rear door of the station wagon.

REV. SUN: I found a small auditorium in L.A. Not the best neighborhood, but it'll do. And I already sold five tickets!

He takes out a box of supplies.

REV. SUN: I brought you a note pad and pen, I assume that will suffice. And lots of Chef Boyardee.

He carries the box to the cabin. Casanova follows.

INT. SECLUDED BEACH - CABIN - DAY

Rev. Sun puts the supplies in the cupboards. He sets out the yellow notepad and a box of pens on the table.

Henny's purse is also on the table. Rev. Sun picks it up.

> REV. SUN: You have company?

Casanova nods.

> REV. SUN: You sly devil! Well. Don't forget you're giving your first lecture a week from Saturday.
>
> CASANOVA: I will be ready.
>
> REV. SUN: You know what this reminds me of? The Chataugua Events in the 19th century, when public lectures were commonplace. In some ways we've lost the intellectual vitality this country used to have.

EXT. SECLUDED BEACH - DAY

Henny is jogging along the wet sand.

EXT. SECLUDED BEACH - CABIN - DAY

The station wagon is pulling up the hill. Casanova is back on the blanket, looking out at the ocean.

Henny returns from her run in time to see the station wagon.

HENNY: Who was that?

CASANOVA: Rev. Sun brought me supplies.

HENNY: Rev. Walter Benjamin Sun of the Church of Metaphysical Truth?

CASANOVA: You know him?

HENNY: I had the misfortune of being on a panel with him once. You're not working for him, are you?

CASANOVA: Is something wrong with that?

HENNY: Only that's he's a charlatan.

CASANOVA: This is my lecture, and I can say anything I want.

HENNY: I think it's time you told me everything.

EXT. SECLUDED BEACH - DAY

They saunter along the wet sand.

CASANOVA: As soon as I have the money, I can pay Larry the Eye and hopefully be able to return home.

He notices that Henny's expression has changed.

CASANOVA: You look so sad.

HENNY: You don't know why?

CASANOVA: I know that it will be sad to part.

HENNY: Sad to part! It's not like you're moving to New York.

CASANOVA: I belong in my own time and place.

HENNY: What about me?

CASANOVA: Are you saying you want to come with me?

HENNY: For the sake of argument, let's say I am. Can that be done?

CASANOVA: Good question. I had to give him a piece of my clothing, something from home. This must be an important part of the magic.

HENNY: Magic, magic, magic. I thought <u>this</u> was our magic.

CASANOVA: You are right: this is wonderful.

HENNY: Then why do you have to leave it?

CASANOVA: We cannot stay here forever.

HENNY: No, but we can live a little longer in the here-and-now, can't we? Amado, we've just begun.

Casanova glares at her.

HENNY: I'm sorry. That just slipped out.

CASANOVA: You still doubt me.

HENNY: It's a real stretch for me to believe you're really Casanova.

CASANOVA: Maybe I would be the same way in your shoes. I will not let this ruin things for us. I forgive you.

HENNY: <u>You</u> forgive <u>me</u>?

CASANOVA: You look surprised.

HENNY: I'll forgive you, too, then.

CASANOVA: For what?

HENNY: For being hooked up with a charlatan. For running away from paradise to go ... God, all the way back to the 18th century! This is madness!

CASANOVA: Why are you so angry?

HENNY: Because I feel cheated!

CASANOVA: I feel blessed.

HENNY: Then that's how we're different.

She turns and starts running back to the cabin. Casanova takes off after her.

EXT. SECLUDED BEACH - CABIN - DAY

Henny is still in front as she reaches the stretch of beach in front of the cabin. Casanova jogs up, out of breath.

HENNY: Are you all right?

Casanova musters a second wind and picks her up. He carries her out into the water and drops her.

EXT. SECLUDED BEACH - CABIN - SUNSET

They sit close on the sand, arms around one another, watching the red globe of the sun slip into the sea.

HENNY: I've made a decision.

CASANOVA: What?

HENNY: I'm not going to think about the future. I'm going to enjoy every moment I have with you like this.

They kiss.

INT. HENNY'S OFFICE - FRONT DESK - DAY

Christiano is talking to Betty Sue.

> CHRISTIANO: It's really important that I find him.
>
> BETTY SUE: All she told me is she was taking a few days off.

The door opens and Henny comes in.

> CHRISTIANO: Where's Amado?
>
> HENNY: Wait for me outside.
>
> CHRISTIANO: This is really important.
>
> HENNY: I'll be right out.

Christiano goes outside.

> HENNY: I'm taking the rest of this week and all next week off. Reschedule my appointments and whatever else you have to do.
>
> BETTY SUE: Ted came by looking for you.
>
> HENNY: Don't tell him where I am.
>
> BETTY SUE: Where are you exactly?
>
> HENNY: Paradise.

Betty Sue looks confused. This is not like her boss.

EXT. COASTAL HIGHWAY - DAY

Henny's car zooms down the highway.

INT. HENNY'S CAR - DAY

Christiano is riding shotgun.

> CHRISTIANO: I don't know how much he told you.
>
> HENNY: A lot. He thinks he's Casanova. He slipped through a worm hole or something.
>
> CHRISTIANO: You know about Larry the Eye?
>
> HENNY: He has magic to help him go back to the 18th century.
>
> CHRISTIANO: Exactly. Only it's more complicated that he thought at first.
>
> HENNY: Chris, you sound like you believe him.
>
> CHRISTIANO: Ah, you know, I go along because I don't want to tilt the delicate balance he's in ... know what I mean?

Henny isn't sure.

EXT. SECLUDED BEACH - CABIN - DAY

Henny's car is parked outside the cabin. Casanova, Christiano and Henny stand nearby.

> CHRISTIANO: Larry the Eye says doing the magic during a full moon will quadruple the chance of success.
>
> CASANOVA: So what is the problem?
>
> CHRISTIANO: The problem was I didn't know how to find you. A full moon isn't that far away, and you still need the money.
>
> CASANOVA: I will have the money.

EXT. SECLUDED BEACH - CABIN - NIGHT

Casanova, Henny and Christiano sit around a campfire on the beach near the cabin. An empty wine bottle lies in the sand, a second one is half full.

> CHRISTIANO: Sex is a basic human need. A basic human right, like food and drink.
>
> HENNY: Which has nothing to do with pornography.
>
> CHRISTIANO: Pornography is like advertising.
>
> HENNY: That demands an explanation!
>
> CHRISTIANO: You turn on TV, you see an

American family sitting in McDonald's having a grand old time, it makes you want to take your kids to the Golden Arches so you can have a really nice family experience, too. It plants the idea in our minds, right? When you watch porno, it's the same thing. You see people aroused and getting it on, so it makes you want to get it on yourself. What's the difference? It's all advertising.

HENNY: I don't even know where to begin to refute that.

CHRISTIANO: Porno's a booming business! It must have something to do with how people want to spend their time.

HENNY: *(to Casanova)* You're being very quiet.

CASANOVA: I think porno is vulgar the same way eating so fast you miss the taste of the meal is vulgar. The destination becomes more important than the journey. Which is backwards.

EXT. SECLUDED BEACH - CABIN - DAY

Henny is sunning herself. She gets off the blanket and enters the cabin.

INT. SECLUDED BEACH - CABIN - DAY

Casanova is working on his lecture when Henny comes in. He's wearing shorts and a tank top.

> HENNY: I'm going out. Need anything at the store?
>
> CASANOVA: I need a break. Let me change and come along.
>
> HENNY: What you're wearing is fine. You look like a native.

EXT. SANTA MONICA - STREET - DAY

Casanova and Henny stroll along, checking out the shops.

Ted drives by in his convertible. He does a double-take when he sees them.

There's a parking place across the street. Ted does a U-turn, cutting off another car, to get it. As he gets out, the other DRIVER rushes out to confront him.

> TED: Sorry. I'm a doctor. I have a medical emergency.

It works. He crosses the street and starts following Henny and Casanova.

He catches up with them and confronts Henny.

> TED: We need to talk.
>
> HENNY: Ted, not now.
>
> TED: Yes, now. I love you.

> HENNY: *(to Casanova)* Can I have fifteen minutes?
>
> CASANOVA: Of course.

He moves off.

Casanova pretends to window shop but glances back to find Ted doing all the talking. Casanova enters a store.

INT. SANTA MONICA - STORE - DAY

Casanova moves among the shelves, passing time. A SECURITY GUARD starts following him.

After looking around, Casanova heads for the door.

> SECURITY GUARD: Hold it, sir.
>
> CASANOVA: Is something the matter?
>
> SECURITY GUARD: Do you play the violin on the boardwalk in Venice?
>
> CASANOVA: Sometimes.
>
> SECURITY GUARD: I thought I recognized you! I caught you a couple times. I really enjoyed it.
>
> CASANOVA: Thank you.

EXT. SANTA MONICA - STREET - DAY

Casanova comes outside and starts back toward Henny. He freezes, a shocked expression on his face.

Henny and Ted are in the middle of a long kiss.

Casanova steps rapidly away.

As soon as his back is turned, Henny pulls away and slaps Ted – hard. But Casanova doesn't see this. He's already lost in the crowd.

EXT. SANTA MONICA - CITY LIMITS - DAY

Casanova reaches the city limits and sticks out his thumb for a ride.

EXT. SANTA MONICA - STREET - DAY

Henny waits for Casanova's return.

Giving up, she moves off to go looking for him.

EXT. SANTA MONICA - ANOTHER STREET - DAY

Cruising through town, Ted sees Henny's car parked at the curb. He pulls into a spot where he can watch it and waits.

EXT. SANTA MONICA - CITY LIMITS - DAY

A car stops and Casanova gets in.

EXT. SANTA MONICA - STREET - DAY

Henny keeps looking for Casanova.

EXT. SANTA MONICA - ANOTHER STREET - DAY

Henny gets into her car alone. She pulls out.

Ted pulls out to follow her.

EXT. COASTAL HIGHWAY - DAY

The car pulls over and Casanova gets out. He sticks out his thumb again.

EXT. COASTAL HIGHWAY - DAY - LATER

Henny's car drives up beside Casanova. She pulls over and leans over to talk through the open window.

>HENNY: Please get in.

Behind her, Ted sees this and slows down.

INT. HENNY'S CAR - DAY

Casanova gets in.

>HENNY: Why didn't you come back?

>CASANOVA: You were kissing him.

HENNY: He was kissing me, but I was <u>not</u> kissing back! I have a bruised hand to prove it.

CASANOVA: I had no idea what was going on.

HENNY: You didn't care enough to come back and find out?

CASANOVA: Who you kiss is none of my business. I thought the best thing to do was leave.

Henny can't believe it. She's speechless.

EXT. COASTAL HIGHWAY - SIDE ROAD - DAY

Henny pulls off the highway to drive down to the cabin.

Ted slowly passes by the dirt turnoff, watching her approach the cabin.

INT. SECLUDED BEACH - CABIN - NIGHT

Casanova and Henny cuddle in bed after making love.

HENNY: You really would have let me go without a fight?

CASANOVA: It is not my place to tell you who you can kiss.

Henny starts to say something and stops. She stares up at the ceiling, looking disappointed.

EXT. SECLUDED BEACH - CABIN - DAY

Casanova and Henny sit in adjacent beach chairs. He works on his lecture. She reads.

EXT. SECLUDED BEACH - NIGHT

They sit at a campfire. Overhead a quarter moon shines.

EXT. SECLUDED BEACH - CABIN - DAY

They are in the beach chairs again, Casanova writing, Henny reading.

Their eyes meet. They smile. But as soon as Casanova goes back to work, Henny's expression changes, she looks concerned about something.

EXT. SECLUDED BEACH - NIGHT

Henny walks the beach alone, thinking. A gibbous moon, less than a week before full, shines overhead.

INT. SECLUDED BEACH - CABIN - NIGHT

Casanova rolls over, reaches for Henny – and finds the bed empty. He gets up.

EXT. SECLUDED BEACH - CABIN - NIGHT

Henny returns to find Casanova sitting outside.

HENNY: I couldn't sleep.

CASANOVA: Neither can I.

HENNY: You were snoring up a storm when I left.

CASANOVA: I woke when I noticed you were gone.

HENNY: Missed me, huh?

CASANOVA: Very much.

HENNY: I'm going to miss going back to the real world.

CASANOVA: So am I.

HENNY: You're still determined to go back to your Venice?

CASANOVA: This is where I belong. I wish there was a way to take you with me.

HENNY: I don't belong there any more than you belong here.

CASANOVA: You are right, of course.

HENNY: It's our curse, isn't it?

CASANOVA: No. It does not mean I love

you any less. Love is more important than convenience.

HENNY: Oh Casanova, Casanova ...

She moves into his arms.

HENNY: You're so much better at this than I am.

EXT. SECLUDED BEACH - CABIN - DAY

Casanova sits in a beach chair, going over his lecture. Henny is swimming in the distance.

Ted appears. He is carrying a flier.

TED: Good afternoon, Casanova. In shorts, you look like any other California beach bum and gigolo. I have your flier.

He reads it aloud.

TED: "History's Greatest Lover Reveals All! The opposite of Past Regression is Future Premonition, and tonight we are honored by a visit from the historic Casanova. Casanova will discuss the Battle of the Sexes from an 18th century perspective. Learn how to increase your Seductive Powers! Discover the Secrets of Sexual Mind Power!" And so on and so forth.

Casanova grabs the flier.

CASANOVA: Where did you get this?

TED: They're everywhere. You obviously have a good marketing team.

CASANOVA: I did not write this!

TED: Oh, of course not.

CASANOVA: This is not what I am lecturing about.

TED: Casanova, whoever you are, I don't give a rat's ass what you're talking about. I'm here to tell you to stop seeing Henny.

CASANOVA: I will stop when it is time to stop.

TED: You'll stop starting right now.

CASANOVA: No.

TED: Then we'll settle this here and now, man to man.

CASANOVA: I do not want to fight you.

TED: Don't tell me the great Casanova is a chicken.

CASANOVA: I have work to do. Please go.

TED: Not until you fight me.

Casanova thinks a moment.

> CASANOVA: If you want to fight, then we shall do it honorably. At sunrise, on Sunday, the morning after my lecture. In the park about a mile up the beach. Christiano will bring the weapons.
>
> TED: Weapons?
>
> CASANOVA: Pistols, for a duel. Perhaps you want to change your mind.
>
> TED: You want a duel, you've got one. Sunrise Sunday it is.

He climbs the hill to his car.

As he disappears out of sight, Henny returns from her swim.

> HENNY: Was that Ted?

He hands her the flier.

> CASANOVA: He gave me this. More lies about me!

INT. CHURCH OF METAPHYSICAL TRUTH - DAY

Casanova storms into the church.

INT. CHURCH OF METAPHYSICAL TRUTH - OFFICE - DAY

Casanova barges in on Rev. Sun having sex with a young FEMALE STUDENT, who sits astride him on a chair. She quickly flees and Rev. Sun composes himself.

Casanova finds a flier on the desk.

>CASANOVA: What is this? This has nothing to do with my lecture!

>REV. SUN: Calm down, calm down. Have I ever said anything about the content of your lecture? Of course not. You are free to talk about whatever you want.

>CASANOVA: Then what is this?

>REV. SUN: Marketing. It will fill the house.

Casanova doesn't know what to say. With a sweep of his hand, he knocks a pile of fliers to the floor.

EXT. SECLUDED BEACH - CABIN - NIGHT

Casanova and Henny sit on the sand under a moon that's almost full.

>CASANOVA: I heard someone use an expression: take the money and run.

>HENNY: If that's the plan, I'd make sure you get paid before you go on stage, not after.

>CASANOVA: You think he would cheat me?

>HENNY: There's another expression we have: better safe than sorry.

EXT. SECLUDED BEACH - CABIN - DAY

Casanova helps Henny unpack groceries from the car.

INT. SECLUDED BEACH - CABIN - DAY

Henny takes a flier from a sack of groceries.

>HENNY: You're not the only Casanova show in town.

She hands him the flier. At the top, it reads: "Tom Snow Productions Presents Casanova Does California."

>HENNY: Are we going?

EXT. L.A. MOVIE HOUSE - NIGHT

A bright spotlight in front of a dilapidated movie house shoots "opening night" beams into the sky.

The theater marquee reads: "One Week Only! Casanova Does California. X-Rated. New erotica from director Tom Snow."

INT. L.A. MOVIE HOUSE - LOBBY - NIGHT

The scene resembles the opening of an art gallery.

Chic, casually formal and arty PEOPLE mingle amidst posters from other Tom Snow movies. Hired HELP circulate with trays of champagne and goodies.

Casanova and Henny stand alone, looking like strangers invited to the wrong party. A white-clad MAN with a tray of snacks passes by, and they help themselves.

> HENNY: "Oh those or-dervies, ain't they neat. Little piece of cheese and a little piece of meat." I can't believe I still remember that. I learned it in college.
>
> CASANOVA: This happens often?
>
> HENNY: I have no idea. I've never been to a porno opening before, believe me. I'm a little shocked, to tell the truth.

In another part of the lobby, Christiano spots them and hurries over. He's wearing a tuxedo top with bermuda shorts. Matching purple.

> CHRISTIANO: I can't believe you're here! I could've gotten you passes but I didn't think you'd come.
>
> HENNY: Checking out the competition.

Christiano looks puzzled.

> HENNY: This is the "other" Casanova show.

Casanova stares at her.

HENNY: It's a joke.

INT. L.A. MOVIE HOUSE - AUDITORIUM - NIGHT

People get seated. Casanova and Henny sit in back.

Tom Snow takes a podium set up beside the screen.

> TOM: Thanks for coming. This is the fourth in my series of Historic Erotica, following my films about Atilla the Hun, Mark Anthony and St. Augustine.

INT. L.A. MOVIE HOUSE - AUDITORIUM - NIGHT - LATER

The movie has begun. On screen, the usual couplings with squeals and groans from Christiano and Sylvia.

In the audience, rapt attention and grins, as if campy wit is being presented.

In the back, Henny and Casanova look like they have indigestion.

> HENNY: I can't watch any more of this.

She gets up to go and Casanova follows.

INT. L.A. MOVIE HOUSE - LOBBY - NIGHT

They pass through the lobby to find Tom Snow at the bar, pacing nervously with a drink in hand.

>TOM: What the hell are you doing here?

>CASANOVA: We're leaving.

>TOM: Good! Go back to Disneyland where you belong! Cocksucking fascists.

EXT. L.A. MOVIE HOUSE - NIGHT

Casanova and Henny come outside and begin walking to her car.

>HENNY: I never knew something like this took place. So many "respectable" people are here.

>CASANOVA: If they expect my lecture to be like this, they'll be disappointed.

>HENNY: What are you going to talk about, if I may ask?

>CASANOVA: That every woman wants to be adored. Every man wants to be respected.

>HENNY: You think it's that simple?

>CASANOVA: Where I come from.

INT. HENNY'S CAR - NIGHT

They are driving along a city street. Henny

discovers that Casanova has been looking at her.

> HENNY: What?
>
> CASANOVA: I want to talk to Larry the Eye.
>
> HENNY: Why not? It's that kind of night.

INT. POOR NEIGHBORHOOD - HOUSE - NIGHT

Larry the Eye lets Casanova and Henny in.

> LARRY THE EYE: You get my message about the full moon?
>
> CASANOVA: I'll be ready.

INT. HOUSE - KITCHEN - NIGHT

They sit at a table, drinking beer.

> LARRY THE EYE: Maybe with a different protocol, I can do something for her. But that's gonna take a lot more research, even if it's possible.
>
> CASANOVA: I was just wondering.
>
> LARRY THE EYE: You know, the magic can only do so much and under the right circumstances. Most people expect us to do whatever we want. No way. Magic has its rules and regulations, just like anything else.

EXT. POOR NEIGHBORHOOD - HOUSE - NIGHT

Larry the Eye walks them out.

> LARRY THE EYE: See you in a few days.
>
> CASANOVA: I'll be here.
>
> LARRY THE EYE: I'm excited. I think it may actually work.

EXT. POOR NEIGHBORHOOD - NIGHT

Casanova and Henny stroll up the street to where her car is parked.

> HENNY: "It may actually work." How can you go through with this?
>
> CASANOVA: I don't see any alternatives.

Henny bites her tongue. They get into her car.

INT. HENNY'S CAR - NIGHT

Henny puts the key in the ignition but doesn't turn it.

> HENNY: Why did you ask him about me?
>
> CASANOVA: I wanted to know if there was a way.

> HENNY: I never said I'd go back with you.
>
> CASANOVA: There'd be no point to try and change your mind unless it was possible.
>
> HENNY: I wish you'd give it more of a chance here. I think we've made progress. Maybe not in all areas, but I think most people are more happy here and now than they were in 1749.
>
> CASANOVA: Were you happier before you met me? I don't think so.
>
> HENNY: That's not fair.

She starts the car.

EXT. SECLUDED BEACH - DAY

Henny jogs along the beach.

EXT. SECLUDED BEACH - CABIN - DAY

She comes up to the cabin. Casanova sits in a deck chair, going over his lecture.

> CASANOVA: How was the run?

She goes inside without answering.

INT. SECLUDED BEACH - CABIN - DAY

Henny looks around, thinking. She fetches her suitcase and opens it.

EXT. SECLUDED BEACH - DAY

Casanova stands at the edge of the water, looking out over the ocean.

EXT. SECLUDED BEACH - CABIN - DAY

He returns to the cabin to find Henny putting a suitcase in the trunk of her car.

>CASANOVA: What are you doing?
>
>HENNY: Going home. Going back to work.
>
>CASANOVA: But we have another day.
>
>HENNY: I'm as ready to say goodbye as I'll ever be.
>
>CASANOVA: Why now?
>
>HENNY: Why not? Goodbye.

She turns before she loses it and gets into the car.

Casanova goes to her window.

>HENNY: Don't ask me to stay.
>
>CASANOVA: I wasn't.
>
>HENNY: Bastard ...

She starts the engine and peels out.

Casanova goes back to his beach chair – and kicks it.

He takes off running down the beach.

EXT. SECLUDED BEACH - DAY

Casanova runs until he is exhausted. He falls onto the sand, gasping for breath.

EXT. OCEAN HIGHWAY - DAY

Henny's car is parked at a phone booth. She's talking to someone.

EXT. HENNY'S OFFICE - DAY

She pulls in front of her office.

INT. HENNY'S OFFICE - FRONT DESK - DAY

Ted is waiting for her. Betty Sue is at her desk.

>HENNY: Thanks for coming, Ted.

She leads Ted toward her office.

>BETTY SUE: Good morning!

>HENNY: Good morning.

INT. HENNY'S OFFICE - OFFICE - DAY

Henny gestures for Ted to sit. She takes the big chair behind her desk.

> HENNY: I guess I've been hard to understand lately.
>
> TED: Very.
>
> HENNY: I'm not going to tell you everything. But I do want your professional advice on something.
>
> TED: Anything.
>
> HENNY: Amado has become dangerous to himself. He needs to be hospitalized. How can I do that?
>
> TED: Is there a relative who would put it in writing?
>
> HENNY: Would that be enough?
>
> TED: It's enough under the law. You have a good relationship with the department. They'll trust your judgment.

She buzzes Betty Sue.

> BETTY SUE: *(on intercom)* Yes?
>
> HENNY: I want Chris here as soon as he can make it. Tell him it's an urgent matter about his parole.

She clicks off.

> HENNY: Thanks, Ted.
>
> TED: Dinner tonight?
>
> HENNY: No.
>
> TED: I see.

He stands.

> HENNY: Call me in a few days.
>
> TED: Seriously?

She manages a smile and nods.

INT. TOM SNOW PRODUCTIONS - BASEMENT - DAY

Sylvia comes halfway down the stairs.

> SYLVIA: Chris, phone call! Sounds important.
>
> CHRISTIANO: I'll take it down here!

He picks up a phone.

> CHRISTIANO: This is Chris.

EXT. SECLUDED BEACH - CABIN - DAY

The sun hangs above the horizon.

Rev. Sun's station wagon pulls up.

INT. SECLUDED BEACH - CABIN - DAY

Casanova is in his native clothes when Rev. Sun enters.

> REV. SUN: You look splendid!

> CASANOVA: How many tickets did we sell?

> REV. SUN: We're sold out. I'm already selling standing room only.

EXT. L.A. - OLD NEIGHBORHOOD - EVENING

The reverend's station wagon passes by the L.A. movie house where Tom Snow's movie is playing.

In the next block, the station wagon pulls in front of an old building.

INT. OLD BUILDING - SMALL AUDITORIUM - EVENING

Rev. Sun leads the way into a small auditorium. Casanova follows.

They climb onto the stage and go behind the curtain.

INT. SMALL AUDITORIUM - DRESSING ROOM - EVENING

They enter a small dressing room. It's dark, dirty, dreary.

> REV. SUN: Quite nice, don't you think?

> CASANOVA: I want my money before I go on.

> REV. SUN: That's not possible. We'll be selling tickets at the door till the last minute.

> CASANOVA: I want a three-hundred dollar advance.

> REV. SUN: You're going to make twice that, but we don't settle accounts until we have a final tally.

> CASANOVA: Then I'm not going on.

He starts out.

> REV. SUN: Wait a minute! I suppose I should understand this since we've never worked together before. You have no reason to trust me until you have reason to trust me. I have two-hundred on me, will that do?

> CASANOVA: Two-fifty. Not a dollar less.

Rev. Sun starts counting out the money.

INT. SMALL AUDITORIUM - ENTRANCE -

NIGHT

A long line of people, mostly men, buy tickets at a table and enter.

INT. SMALL AUDITORIUM - NIGHT

The small auditorium, which holds about 300, is packed to standing-room only capacity.

INT. SMALL AUDITORIUM - DRESSING ROOM - NIGHT

Christiano enters.

    CHRISTIANO: We're in deep shit.

    CASANOVA: What's the matter?

    CHRISTIANO: Never trust a shrink you go to bed with. She double-crossed you.

    CASANOVA: What happened?

    CHRISTIANO: She forced me to sign your commitment papers. They're going to pick you up right after the lecture and haul you off to the booby hatch. Fortunately, I have an idea. I'll be you, and you get the hell out of here and get your ass over to Larry the Eye's.

    CASANOVA: How can you be me?

    CHRISTIANO: I'm an actor.

CASANOVA: What will you say?

CHRISTIANO: I'll wing it. They won't know the difference, trust me.

CASANOVA: I was going to start with a poem. I'll write it down for you.

CHRISTIANO: What about sunrise? The duel still on?

CASANOVA: Yes.

CHRISTIANO: Won't you be gone by then?

CASANOVA: To be honest, I hope I am. The duel is a stupid idea.

EXT. OLD BUILDING - NIGHT

Casanova, in Christiano's shorts and tank top, rushes out of the building. He hurries off, looking up the street for a cab.

INT. SMALL AUDITORIUM - DRESSING ROOM - NIGHT

Rev. Sun finds Christiano wearing Casanova's native costume.

REV. SUN: Where's Casanova?

CHRISTIANO: You're looking at him.

REV. SUN: He cheated me!

CHRISTIANO: With all due respect, do you think anybody in the audience gives a rat's ass who talks to them, as long as they hear what they want to hear?

REV. SUN: You can do this?

CHRISTIANO: I'm an actor, I can do anything.

EXT. L.A. MOVIE HOUSE - NIGHT

Casanova passes by the movie house where Tom Snow's movie is playing. A small group of female protesters is picketing outside.

Among the picketers is Sharon. She runs up to him.

SHARON: We tried to crash the entrance but there weren't enough of us to force our way in.

Casanova gets an idea.

CASANOVA: Don't go away. I'll be right back.

He runs back toward the old building.

INT. SMALL AUDITORIUM - NIGHT

Two UNDERCOVER DEPUTIES stand in the back of the auditorium, looking very official. They look over the packed house with expressions of stoic menace.

INT. SMALL AUDITORIUM - STAGE - NIGHT

Christiano comes out to applause and cheers. He bows very theatrically, then goes behind the podium.

> CHRISTIANO: We're here to talk about sex. Right?

Yells and applause.

> CHRISTIANO: Great. I'll start with a poem. *(reading)* "If questioning would make us wise, / No eyes would ever gaze in eyes; / If all our tale were told in speech, / No mouths would wander each to each."

INT. SMALL AUDITORIUM - NIGHT

In the back, the deputies listen.

> CHRISTIANO: *(O.S., reading)* "Were spirits free from mortal mesh / And love not bound in hearts of flesh, / No aching breasts would yearn to meet / And find their ecstasy complete."

One deputy shrugs to the other, What the hell is this all about?

INT. SMALL AUDITORIUM - STAGE -

NIGHT

Christiano continues reading when Casanova rushes onto the stage, interrupting him.

> CASANOVA: I need men to come with me to a porno movie! *(to Christiano)* Tell them to come with me.

> CHRISTIANO: Let's go to a porno movie!

Hundreds of men get to their feet, cheering and yelling.

EXT. OLD BUILDING - NIGHT

Casanova leads hundreds of men out of the building and onto the street. They start marching toward the nearby movie house.

EXT. L.A MOVIE HOUSE - NIGHT

They reach the movie house, where the picketing ladies are outside. Seeing all the men and not knowing what is going on, the women make room for them to pass by.

Sharon sees that Casanova is leading the mob and smiles.

Casanova leads the men to the entrance.

INT. L.A MOVIE HOUSE - NIGHT

The men storm inside the movie house. A few

GUARDS try to stop them at first but quickly understand the situation and retreat.

Tom Snow is at a portable bar.

> TOM: What the hell? Get out of my movie!

The mob ignores him, storming into the auditorium. Casanova slips out of their way.

Tom sees him.

> TOM: You did this!

> CASANOVA: I'd love to have a drink with you, but I'm late to an appointment.

He moves past the advancing mob for the exit.

INT. L.A MOVIE HOUSE - AUDITORIUM - NIGHT

Men fill the aisles of the movie house. And more. And more.

The situation quickly turns chaotic, the movie ignored in the packed confusion of all the men rushing into the auditorium.

The movie is turned off. The house lights come on. The situation is more chaotic than ever.

EXT. L.A MOVIE HOUSE - NIGHT

Sharon runs up to Casanova.

SHARON: Thank you, so much!

CASANOVA: The Casanova in that movie is a lie. I have my reputation to protect.

He hurries off, leaving Sharon puzzled.

INT. POOR NEIGHBORHOOD - HOUSE - KITCHEN - NIGHT

Larry the Eye holds up a small bottle filled with colored liquid.

LARRY THE EYE: Have a safe trip.

Casanova takes the bottle, looking intensely at the liquid.

EXT. OCEAN HIGHWAY - NIGHT

Casanova, who has been hitch-hiking, runs to a pick-up truck that has stopped for him. He climbs inside and the truck takes off.

EXT. SECLUDED BEACH - CABIN - NIGHT

Casanova walks down the dirt road to the cabin. The full moonlight is high and casts his shadow.

He continues onto the beach.

He untwists the cap off the small bottle. He raises the bottle to the full moon, as if making a toast.

He drinks down the colored liquid in one gulp.

He takes a deep breath, waiting. Nothing happens.

INT. HENNY'S HOUSE - BEDROOM - NIGHT

Henny tosses and turns, unable to sleep.

INT. SECLUDED BEACH - CABIN - NIGHT

Casanova tosses and turns, unable to sleep.

INT. HENNY'S HOUSE - BEDROOM - NIGHT

Henny gives up and rolls out of bed.

INT. SECLUDED BEACH - CABIN - NIGHT

Casanova is snoring.

Henny tip-toes in. She undresses and crawls in bed beside him. He stirs.

> CASANOVA: What are–?

She puts a finger on his lips, hushing him. They kiss and begin to make love.

EXT. OCEAN HIGHWAY - PARK - SUNRISE

Ted's convertible pulls into the park. Christiano is waiting for him.

TED: Where is he?

CHRISTIANO: He'll be here.

INT. SECLUDED BEACH - CABIN - SUNRISE

Casanova, dressed in his frills, bends to kiss Henny on the forehead. She makes a little sound.

EXT. SECLUDED BEACH - CABIN - SUNRISE

He comes out and heads up the beach toward the park.

EXT. PARK - BEACH - SUNRISE

They see Casanova approaching up the beach.

CHRISTIANO: Here he comes.

INT. SECLUDED BEACH - CABIN - SUNRISE

Henny wakes to find the bed empty. She gets up.

EXT. SECLUDED BEACH - CABIN - SUNRISE

She comes outside.

HENNY: Casanova?

She looks up the beach and makes out a figure in the distance. She heads out in that direction.

EXT. PARK - SUNRISE

Casanova and Ted are back to back, each holding up a small pistol.

> CHRISTIANO: Ten steps, turn and fire. Are you ready?
>
> CASANOVA: Ready.
>
> TED: Ready.
>
> CHRISTIANO: One ... two ...

At each count they take a step.

> CHRISTIANO: Three ... four ...

EXT. BEACH - NEAR PARK - SUNRISE

Henny gets closer. She realizes what is going on. She starts running.

EXT. PARK - SUNRISE

Christiano continues the count.

> CHRISTIANO: Seven ... eight ...

Henny is close enough to be heard.

> CHRISTIANO: Nine ...
>
> HENNY: Casanova!

CHRISTIANO: Ten!

HENNY: Casanova!

At ten, Casanova hears Henny and turns. At the same time, Ted fires and hits him. Casanova falls to the sand.

Henny screams and runs up to him. Christiano runs to him as well.

Ted stares at what he's done.

Henny takes Casanova in her arms, embracing him.

Casanova stirs. He opens his eyes.

HENNY: Casanova ...

With difficulty, Casanova reaches into his pocket. He brings out a coin, which he gives to Henny.

Henny looks at the coin. It's an old Italian coin.

CASANOVA: It's from the old country ... in case you need something ...

He closes his eyes.

SUPER

"Venice, Italy. Summer, 1749."

EXT. VENICE - A FIELD - NIGHT

Rosabel cradles Casanova in her arms in the exact same position that Henny was holding him on the beach. Looking on is MATTEO BRAGADIN, 50s, a nobleman.

Casanova opens his eyes.

> CASANOVA: Rosabel ... Matteo ... what happened?

Bragadin stoops and offers a vial of medicine.

> BRAGADIN: Take this ... it will counteract the other ...

Casanova does.

> BRAGADIN: Thank God the girl fetched me in time. I've made arrangements for you to leave Venice.
>
> CASANOVA: Why?
>
> BRAGADIN: Because if you don't, you'll be arrested. I brought you a fresh horse. A stage leaves for Rome first thing in the morning. Are you strong enough to ride?
>
> CASANOVA: I think so.

EXT. VENICE - A FIELD - NIGHT - LATER

Casanova is on the horse. He bends low to kiss Rosabel.

> ROSABEL: I love you so much.
>
> CASANOVA: Then don't forget me.
>
> BRAGADIN: God speed, my boy. Send me a letter when you get settled.

Casanova nods and spurs the horse. He's away in a gallop.

EXT. VENICE - POOR NEIGHBORHOOD - HOUSE - DAY (PRESENT)

Henny pulls up in front of Larry the Eye's house. She gets out and hurries to the door.

Larry the Eye opens the door. Henny says something to him, and then he lets her in.

INT. HOUSE - KITCHEN - DAY

Larry the Eye leads Henny into the kitchen.

> LARRY THE EYE: I can't do this unless you have something from–

She's ahead of him. She holds out the old Italian coin.

> LARRY THE EYE: That should do the trick.

EXT. STAGE STATION - SUNRISE (BACK TO HISTORIC VENICE, ITALY)

A stage is being boarded as Casanova races up on

the horse. He jumps off and hurries to the STAGE DRIVER.

> CASANOVA: Is it too late to board?
>
> STAGE DRIVER: You got fare?

Casanova pays him with an old coin like the one he gave Henny.

> STAGE DRIVER: You have the last seat.

INT. STAGE COACH - SUNRISE

Casanova climbs up into the stage. An ELDERLY COUPLE sleep next to the only vacant seat.

Across from the vacant seat is a beautiful YOUNG WOMAN. She is a dead-ringer for Henny. The young woman's GUARDIAN dozes next to her, large enough to take up two seats.

Casanova squeezes in and exchanges a smile with the young woman.

> CASANOVA: Just made it.
>
> YOUNG WOMAN: I guess you did.
>
> CASANOVA: I'm Giacomo Casanova.

He offers his hand.

> YOUNG WOMAN: Henriette. But everyone calls me Henny.

She offers her hand and he takes it, then bends forward and kisses it.

> CASANOVA: Have we met before?
>
> YOUNG WOMAN: I don't recall when ... but it feels like we have.
>
> CASANOVA: I have the same feeling. I always trust my feelings.
>
> YOUNG WOMAN: Are you going all the way to Rome?
>
> CASANOVA: Are you?
>
> YOUNG WOMAN: Yes.
>
> CASANOVA: Then so am I.
>
> YOUNG WOMAN: What will you do there?
>
> CASANOVA: Play the violin, I hope. I'm auditioning for the orchestra.
>
> YOUNG WOMAN: I play the cello.
>
> CASANOVA: Maybe we'll have the opportunity to play together sometime.
>
> YOUNG WOMAN: I'd like that.

The guardian snorts herself awake, then settles down back to sleep.

Henny hides a giggle with the palm of her hand.

Casanova winks at her. She blushes.

He blows her a kiss. She blushes even more.

EXT. STAGE STATION - SUNRISE

The stage driver snaps the reins, and the stage coach moves off.

INT. STAGE COACH - SUNRISE

The jolt of starting up has thrown Casanova and Henny together. They kiss. And stay kissed ...

EXT. STAGE STATION - SUNRISE

... as the stage coach bounces along toward the horizon.

FADE OUT.

LOVE IN THE RUINS

*(Based on the novel "Love At Ground Zero"
By Charles Deemer)*

Wes and Hayaam, two students, an American and a Muslim, become attracted to one another in the tense climate of post-9/11 America. Family, friends and history itself oppose their growing love. A retelling of the archetypal "Romeo and Juliet" love story for an Age of Terror.

FADE IN:

EXT. NEW YORK - WORLD TRADE CENTER - DAY

Two Muslim women approach the complex of buildings of the World Trade Center. They are HAYAAM and AREEBAH, both early 20s, dressed in traditional Muslim attire (hijab).

Hayaam wears very bright colors, Areebah more subdued ones.

They head for the south World Trade Center tower.

SUPER: "8:30 a.m."

EXT. WORLD TRADE CENTER - STREET - DAY

A cab stops near the complex.

Getting out are WES HARDING, early 20s, and his brother, MIKE, a little older. They are dressed casually in slacks, sports coats.

They head for the entrance into the south tower.

> WES: How long you gonna be?

> MIKE: He has a meeting at nine. I'll meet you in the coffee shop.

WES: How's he like being a stock broker?

MIKE: Jimmy likes making money.

WES: So do you, big brother.

INT. WORLD TRADE CENTER - SOUTH TOWER - DAY

Wes and Mike enter the south tower building.

Wes heads for a coffee shop on the ground floor. Mike heads for the elevator.

Standing at the elevator are Hayaam and Areebah.

INT. WORLD TRADE CENTER - COFFEE SHOP - DAY

Wes brings a cup of coffee and donut to a table. A folded newspaper is under his arm.

INT. WORLD TRADE CENTER - ELEVATOR - DAY

On the crowded elevator are Mike, Hayaam and Areebah.

The elevator stops, the door opens, and Hayaam and Areebah step off.

Mike continues up.

INT. WORLD TRADE CENTER - COFFEE SHOP - DAY

Wes is reading the paper.

Suddenly there is a loud sound, a great crash outside somewhere.

Customers go to windows, looking outside to see what is going on.

Wes looks up from the paper but stays at the table.

> CUSTOMER: My God, the north tower is on fire!

More people go to the windows to look outside. Wes joins them.

INT. WORLD TRADE CENTER - OFFICE - DAY

Mike and JIMMY stand at the window of Jimmy's high office, looking out at the flames consuming the north tower.

INT. WORLD TRADE CENTER - INSURANCE COUNTER - DAY

Hayaam and Areebah stand at the counter of an insurance company. They look frightened and confused as people rush past them to see what has happened outside.

INT. WORLD TRADE CENTER - COFFEE SHOP - DAY

Wes comes back to his table. He seems uncertain what to do.

Around him, everyone is gawking out at the fire next door. Everyone is talking at once.

Wes looks at his watch.

Suddenly there is another loud crash, this one even louder than before.

The room rocks, as if hit by an earthquake.

People scream. People start moving for the exits.

Wes abandons what is left of his coffee and the newspaper and joins the rush to get out.

EXT. WORLD TRADE CENTER - SOUTH TOWER - DAY

Wes comes outside. He sees the flames rising from the north tower.

He looks straight up and sees flames rising from the south tower as well. Dark smoke billows everywhere.

A look of realization on Wes' face: Mike is still in there.

Wes turns and fights the flow of people rushing outside, trying to get back inside the building.

INT. WORLD TRADE CENTER - DAY

Wes manages to slip inside against the human current. He sees a stairway and heads for it.

INT. WORLD TRADE CENTER - STAIRS - DAY

People are rushing downstairs. Wes fights his way against the flow, heading up.

A SECURITY GUARD meets Wes on the stairs.

> SECURITY GUARD: You can't go up, sir. We're evacuating the building.
>
> WES: My brother's up there!
>
> SECURITY GUARD: I'm sure he's on his way down. Come along, sir.

Wes gives in and heads down again. He lets the security guard move ahead of him, then turns and heads up again.

But it's hopeless, the stairway is too crowded, there's too much chaos around him.

He stops and presses himself against a wall in a stairwell, letting the crowd rush past him, gathering his thoughts, catching his breath.

He looks up the stairs to find more and more people heading down. Maybe Mike will be one of them.

He gives in and starts down again.

He passes an open doorway at a floor level and hears a woman's cry for help. There's something in the tone of voice that stops him.

He moves to the door and steps into a hallway.

INT. WORLD TRADE CENTER - HALLWAY - DAY

Wes looks up and down the hallway. The cry for help comes again. He moves in its direction.

He finds the two women in Muslim dress, Hayaam and Areebah. Hayaam is sitting on the floor, Areebah bending over her. (Their English is heavily accented.)

>AREEBAH: She can't walk! She twisted her ankle!

>WES: Okay, you'll be alright. Take my hand.

Hayaam grasps Wes' hand, and he pulls her to her feet.

>WES: Can you walk at all?

Hayaam takes a test step but falters. Wes holds her up.

>WES: Okay, here we go.

He lifts her up in his arms.

> WES: You okay?

> HAYAAM: Yes.

Wes carries her, heading for the stairs. Areebah follows.

INT. WORLD TRADE CENTER - STAIRS - DAY

Wes moves back into the stairwell. He turns to make sure Areebah is behind him.

> WES: Grab my arm.

Areebah does.

Wes, carrying Hayaam, enters the rush of people heading down the stairs.

People cough from heavy gasoline fumes. Some hold handkerchiefs over their mouths.

Water flows down the stairs from broken pipes.

EXT. WORLD TRADE CENTER - DAY

Wes, Hayaam and Areebah come outside. Everyone gasps for air.

Areebah releases her grip.

Wes carefully sets Hayaam down. She supports

herself on her good leg.

> WES: I have to go back inside. Will you be okay?
>
> HAYAAM: Yes. Thank you so much.
>
> WES: No problem.

Hayaam offers her hand.

> HAYAAM: I am Hayaam. This is my cousin, Areebah.
>
> WES: I'm Wes. You work here?
>
> HAYAAM: Oh no, I'm a student. And you work here?
>
> WES: I go to NYU.
>
> HAYAAM: Really? So do I.
>
> WES: I have to go. My brother's in there somewhere.

He heads back to the entrance.

> HAYAAM: *(after him)* Thank you!

Wes fights his way against the flow again.

EXT. CEMETERY - DAY

A GATHERING of people stands at a fresh grave. A

casket is lowered into the ground.

In the gathering are Wes, his father WALTER HARDING and his mother EVELYN. And other FRIENDS and RELATIVES.

INT. HARDING HOME - DAY

A reception after the funeral. A long table filled with food. An open bar.

In a circle of MEN, Wes' UNCLE FRANK is holding court.

> UNCLE FRANK: It's worse than Pearl Harbor because it's right here at home, right in our own back yard. This will change everything, see if I'm not right. This is a new kind of war, and we damn well better be ready to show the world we have another great generation.

Wes, listening at the edge of the circle, moves away.

INT. HARDING HOME - MIKE'S ROOM - DAY

Wes is alone in his brother's room. Signs that it hasn't been lived in for a while — boxes stored on the bed.

Wes goes to a wall where there is an NYU pennant and a photo of Mike in a football uniform from high school.

ROGER, 20s, appears in the doorway.

>ROGER: You okay?
>
>WES: Well as can be expected.
>
>ROGER: You want to get out of here? Go for a ride or something?
>
>WES: I'll be okay.
>
>ROGER: I could use some air.

EXT. NEW YORK - NEIGHBORHOOD STREET - DAY

Wes and Roger walk through the urban neighborhood.

>WES: You have any Arab friends?
>
>ROGER: That's an interesting question. You mean, do I think they're spies? Yeah, if I had any, I'd be worried about it.
>
>WES: When it happened, I went crazy, thinking I could find Mike somehow ... I didn't even know what floor his buddy's office was on ... anyway, I heard a call for help and followed it. There were two Arab women, and one of them had sprained her ankle. I carried her out.

They walk a moment in silence.

> ROGER: And ...?
>
> WES: And what?
>
> ROGER: Is there a point to this story?
>
> WES: Not really. I was just wondering how she must be feeling.

Roger gives him a strange look.

> WES: What's wrong?
>
> ROGER: Thousands of people got killed. Your brother. Why are you bringing up an Arab woman with a sprained ankle?

Wes can't answer him.

EXT. NYU CAMPUS - DAY

Wes is walking across campus. Ahead he sees a woman in traditional Muslim clothing.

He hesitates, then rushes up behind her. He clears his throat, and she turns. It's not Hayaam.

> ARAB WOMAN: Yes?
>
> WES: I'm sorry. I thought you were someone else.

INT. NYU CAMPUS - LIBRARY - DAY

Wes is studying a book at a table.

Hayaam comes in on crutches, wearing her usual brightly colored hijab.

Wes looks up and sees her. He smiles but she doesn't see him.

Hayaam disappears in the stacks.

Wes closes the book and gets up. He follows her.

INT. LIBRARY - STACKS - DAY

Hayaam is having trouble maneuvering both her crutches and a book she's trying to get high off the shelf.

Wes appears.

> WES: Let me.

He takes down the book for her.

> HAYAAM: Thank you.

She recognizes him.

> HAYAAM: Hello! I was wondering if I might run into you.

> WES: Same here. How's the ankle?

> HAYAAM: I'm supposed to let it rest. Not so easy when you have things to do.

Wes looks at the book, which he's still holding.

> WES: Immanuel Kant ... I'm impressed.
>
> HAYAAM: Don't be. I'm only reading it because I have to. I'm a philosophy major. He's actually quite boring.
>
> WES: I think I remember that. Listen, if you're not busy, I was about to grab a cup of coffee.
>
> HAYAAM: Tea would be nice.

INT. NYU CAMPUS - COFFEE SHOP - DAY

Wes and Hayaam sit at a table. Wes is telling his story.

> WES: I shouldn't feel guilty, I know there's nothing I could've done.
>
> HAYAAM: Of course there wasn't.
>
> WES: It's just that ...
>
> HAYAAM: What?
>
> WES: I felt so helpless. So powerless.
>
> HAYAAM: You weren't helpless at all. You helped me. You probably saved my life. I could've still been in there when the tower fell.

Wes looks surprised. This never occurred to him.

>WES: You think so?

>HAYAAM: Yes. I think you are my life saver.

EXT. NYU CAMPUS - DAY

They move slowly across campus. Hayaam, of course, uses her crutches.

>WES: Where are you from?

>HAYAAM: Indonesia.

>WES: Indonesia.

>HAYAAM: You thought I am Arab, right?

>WES: I guess I did.

>HAYAAM: There are more Muslims in Indonesia than in any other country.

>WES: I didn't know that.

Ahead a crowd of FRATERNITY BROTHERS have circled around a foreign student. This is ABDUL-HAKEEM. They are taunting him.

Wes and Hayaam get close enough that she recognizes it's her brother who is being taunted.

>HAYAAM: Abdul!

She gets the crutches into high gear.

> WES: What is it?

Wes hurries after her.

Abdul tries to move out of the circle around him but the fraternity brothers keep blocking his way.

> FRATERNITY BRO #1: Foreign fuck.

> FRATERNITY BRO #2: Arab asshole.

Hayaam takes a crutch and holds it over her head, a gesture of threat.

> HAYAAM: Let him go!

The fraternity boys find her gesture amusing.

> FRATERNITY BRO #2: Hey, sweetie pie. What do you plan to do with that?

> FRATERNITY BRO #3: Why you got that scarf covering your hair? I bet you got pretty hair.

He reaches for the scarf and Hayaam strikes his arm with a crutch.

Wes intervenes.

> WES: Hey, fellas, what's going on?

> FRATERNITY BRO #1: You with her?

In the confusion, Abdul has slipped out of the circle.

> ABDUL-HAKEEM: Hayaam, this is not your fight.
>
> FRATERNITY BRO #2: Who said anything about a fight? We just want you to go the fuck home where you belong.
>
> ABDUL-HAKEEM: I study here, so today this is my home.

He grabs Hayaam and starts moving away.

Wes isn't sure what to do.

> FRATERNITY BRO #3: Something we can help you with?
>
> WES: No ... thanks, no ...

He follows Hayaam and catches up with her and Abdul.

> WES: What was that about?
>
> ABDUL-HAKEEM: *(to Hayaam)* Who is this?
>
> HAYAAM: He's the one I told you about, who saved my life. *(to Wes)* My brother, Abdul-Hakeem.

> WES: Nice to meet you. I'm Wes.

He offers his hand. Abdul hesitates before taking it.

> ABDUL-HAKEEM: I give you my gratitude for helping my sister.

> WES: I'm sorry for what happened back there.

> ABDUL-HAKEEM: Your countrymen decided I am a terrorist.

Wes can't find the words to reply.

> ABDUL-HAKEEM: Hayaam, we must go.

She smiles at Wes.

> HAYAAM: Thank you for the tea.

> WES: Maybe we can do it again soon.

Hayaam smiles.

Abdul quickly leads his sister away.

INT. HARDING HOME - DINING ROOM - NIGHT

Seated at the dinner table are Wes, Walter and Evelyn. Evelyn is just picking at her food.

Suddenly Evelyn starts sobbing.

EVELYN: I'm sorry ...

She gets up from the table.

WALTER: Evelyn, it's okay.

EVELYN: Stop saying everything is okay!

She hurries off.

WALTER: I meant crying is okay.

WES: I know.

They go back to eating.

WES: Dad ... do you know any Muslims?

WALTER: We used to have a lawyer in the firm who was Muslim. Why?

WES: If he was still in the firm, would you suspect him of being a terrorist?

WALTER: Of course not. Why do you ask?

WES: There was a scuffle at school today, some jock types hassling a student from Indonesia.

WALTER: There's going to be a lot of that, I'm afraid. Stupidity and patriotism make a volatile mix.

Wes nods and eats.

EXT. HARDING HOME - BASKETBALL COURT - DAY

There's a basketball hoop and makeshift court along the driveway. Wes and Roger are shooting baskets.

> WES: I ran into Hayaam on campus.

Roger looks puzzled.

> WES: The girl I carried out of the tower before it collapsed.

Roger stops dribbling.

> ROGER: Don't tell me you're interested in an Arab girl.

> WES: She's from Indonesia. We had coffee. No big deal.

> ROGER: Then why are you talking about her?

Good question. Wes grabs the ball and dribbles for a lay up. Wes tosses Roger the ball.

> ROGER: Do me a favor. If you get involved with this girl, keep it to yourself.

He takes a shot.

INT. NYU CAMPUS - ART STUDIO - DAY

Wes is working on an abstract painting, full of bright colors.

Out the window, he sees Hayaam hobbling across campus on her crutches.

He thinks a minute, then puts down his brush.

EXT. NYU CAMPUS - DAY

Wes catches up with Hayaam on the front steps just before she enters a building.

>WES: Hey.
>
>HAYAAM: Hello.
>
>WES: You have a class?
>
>HAYAAM: Yes, that boring Mr. Kant.
>
>WES: And afterwards?
>
>HAYAAM: I have three hours before my next class.
>
>WES: Time for tea?
>
>HAYAAM: Since when do you drink tea?
>
>WES: Tea for you, coffee for me. Meet you in the coffee shop?

HAYAAM: That would be nice.

She gives him a big smile and enters the building.

Wes moves off.

From a distance, Abdul watches him go. He looks concerned.

INT. NYU CAMPUS - COFFEE SHOP - DAY

Wes sits alone at a table. He looks at his watch. Thirty minutes after the hour. She's very late.

He scoots back his chair, getting ready to go.

Hayaam rushes into the coffee shop as best she can on crutches. She sees Wes and gets to the table just as he steps away.

> HAYAAM: I'm sorry I'm late. You have a class?
>
> WES: No.
>
> HAYAAM: You're angry with me. I don't blame you.
>
> WES: No, I'm glad you made it.
>
> HAYAAM: What is it you say? Better late than never?
>
> WES: Yes, better late than never.

They sit down at the table. An awkward silence.

> HAYAAM: You're mad at me.
>
> WES: No.
>
> HAYAAM: You look upset.
>
> WES: I'm not, really. Do you want to take a walk? I guess it would be hard for you ...
>
> HAYAAM: No, I would like to.

A SERIES OF SHOTS - WES & HAYAAM

Wes and Hayaam begin spending a lot of time together.

On campus:

– They walk together between classes, Hayaam on her crutches.

– They study in the library together.

– They have lunch in the coffee shop.

– Wes shows her his painting-in-progress in the art studio.

In the city:

– They window shop.

– They buy ice cream at a corner stand.

-- They walk in a city park.

EXT. NEW YORK - SIDEWALK CAFE - DAY

Wes and Hayaam are having lunch at a sidewalk cafe. The crutches lean against the table.

> HAYAAM: I take my exam next week.
>
> WES: You have midterms already?
>
> HAYAAM: Not at University. For my citizenship.

This is news to Wes.

> HAYAAM: I know, I didn't tell you before.
>
> WES: Hayaam, I think that's great. Then you're staying here.?
>
> HAYAAM: That's the plan, yes. My father will be joining Abdul and me next month, we hope. My mother died last year.
>
> WES: I'm sorry.
>
> HAYAAM: I think my father doesn't approve of me becoming an American, but he knows how strong willed I am. I will be a citizen of two countries, Indonesia and United States.

She sees something in Wes' expression.

HAYAAM: What is that look?

WES: What look?

HAYAAM: Like you don't believe I'm strong willed.

WES: I guess I haven't noticed that in you yet. I thought ...

HAYAAM: Yes?

WES: Muslim women were more, you know, submissive to men than in the west.

HAYAAM: Why do you think this?

WES: Like how they walk behind the men ... like how you dress ...

HAYAAM: Do I walk behind you?

WES: No, you don't. But you do wear traditional dress.

HAYAAM: Because it's liberating.

WES: Liberating?

HAYAAM: Why does this amuse you? I dress like this because I refuse to be looked at as a sex object. I refuse to be a part of the sexism that is the basis of gender relations in the west. If you want a relationship with me, you must start by engaging my mind. There are no physical distractions. This is why the hijab is liberating.

Wes is at a loss for words.

>	HAYAAM: What are you thinking?

>	WES: I never thought about it that way.

INT. NYU CAMPUS - GYM - BASKETBALL COURT - DAY

Wes and Roger shooting baskets.

>	ROGER: That is the biggest crock I've ever heard.

>	WES: There's a logic to it. Put yourself in the shoes of a woman.

>	ROGER: Listen to you. You're thinking with your cock, white man.

INT. NYU CAMPUS - LOCKER ROOM - DAY

They are dressing after their workout.

>	ROGER: Have you nailed her yet?

>	WES: We're just friends.

>	ROGER: Bullshit. You can't talk about anyone else.

> WES: Okay, I find her fascinating. But we're just friends.
>
> ROGER: Do I detect a certain sadness in your tone?
>
> WES: She's a Muslim.
>
> ROGER: Exactly. You nail her, and they stone her in the street, right? Then her brother tracks you down and cuts off your dick.

Wes stares at him.

INT. NEW YORK - BOOKSTORE - DAY

Wes looks for a book on the shelves. He finds it.

It's called "An Introduction to Islam." He takes it.

On his way to the cash register, he passes a table of books. A title catches his eye: "The Rubiyat of Omar Khayam."

EXT. NYU CAMPUS - DAY

Wes catches up with Hayaam, who is carefully stepping across campus. She is finally off crutches.

> WES: Hi.
>
> HAYAAM: Hello.
>
> WES: When did you get off crutches?

HAYAAM: Yesterday. If I am careful, I'm fine.

They walk a moment in silence.

WES: I think I owe you an apology.

HAYAAM: I don't understand.

WES: I know we've never really been alone together ... I mean, we always spend time together in public places ... but I didn't realize it was against your religion to date. I thought we've been, you know, sort of dating. I didn't mean any disrespect.

HAYAAM: You think I am forbidden to be alone with you?

WES: I've been reading about Islam. It says you don't date or spend time alone with the opposite sex.

HAYAAM: I see. This is like my hijab, another example of my repression. You must feel so sorry for me.

WES: I'm not trying to make you angry. I'm trying to apologize.

HAYAAM: You are making me angry! I consider myself a feminist. Yes, a Muslim feminist! Whatever book you are reading, I think you are getting bad information.

She moves off, leaving Wes confused.

INT. NYU CAMPUS - LIBRARY - DAY

Hayaam is studying. Wes appears.

He sits down next to her and speaks in low tones.

> WES: How's the studying for citizenship coming?
>
> HAYAAM: Good.
>
> WES: I'd be glad to help. Quiz you, whatever you need.
>
> HAYAAM: You would do this?
>
> WES: I'd like to.
>
> HAYAAM: Even if we must be alone to do this?
>
> WES: I deserve that. Yes, even if we are alone.
>
> HAYAAM: Then yes, you can help me.

INT. HARDING HOME - DINING ROOM - NIGHT

The family at dinner. No one speaks.

Evelyn gets up and exits to the kitchen.

> WES: I've been seeing the Muslim woman I told you about. She's studying to become a citizen. I thought I'd help her study.
>
> WALTER: Is that a question?
>
> WES: I was wondering if it would be okay to bring her here. I mean, the way mom feels and everything.
>
> WALTER: Of course you can bring her here.
>
> WES: Thanks, Dad.

EXT. HARDING HOME - DAY

Wes and Hayaam approach the house.

> HAYAAM: I think I'm nervous. I don't meet people well.
>
> WES: Trust me, my parents are great. A friend of mine is a friend of theirs.

They walk onto the porch.

A NEIGHBOR watering the lawn next door gets an eyeful of Hayaam in her traditional clothing.

INT. HARDING HOME - LIVING ROOM - DAY

Walter looks out the front window, seeing Wes and Hayaam reach the porch. Evelyn stands behind him.

> WALTER: Well, they're here.
>
> EVELYN: I'm not ready for this.

She hurries off. Walter starts to say something but doesn't.

INT. HARDING HOME - FOYER - DAY

The door opens, and Hayaam and Wes enter.

Walter is waiting to greet them.

> WES: Dad, this is Hayaam.
>
> WALTER: I thought it must be. It's very nice to meet you, Hayaam.
>
> HAYAAM: It is a pleasure to meet you.
>
> WES: I'm helping her study for her citizenship exam.
>
> WALTER: I believe you mentioned that.
>
> WES: Is mom around?
>
> WALTER: She seems to have gone off on an errand.
>
> WES: We'll be in my room.

Wes gestures to the stairway, and they leave.

INT. HARDING HOME - KITCHEN - DAY

Walter comes into the kitchen.

> WALTER: Evelyn?

He sees her out the kitchen window. She's standing alone in the back yard. Her back is to him. She appears to be crying.

INT. HARDING HOME - WES' ROOM - DAY

Hayaam sits at Wes' desk. Wes sits on the edge of the bed. He has a booklet in his hand.

> WES: "Give me liberty or give me death!"

> HAYAAM: Patrick Henry.

Wes smiles.

> WES: "These are the times that try men's souls."

> HAYAAM: Thomas Paine.

> WES: You know this stuff better than I do.

> HAYAAM: Here's one that's not in the book. "No taxation without representation."

> WES: I know that one.

He thinks a minute.

WES: Samuel Adams.

HAYAAM: Samuel Adams was his law clerk.

WES: Really? Hmm ...

HAYAAM: John Adams called this man "the First Patriot."

WES: My mind's gone blank.

HAYAAM: James Otis.

WES: James Otis?

HAYAAM: Yes. You remember now?

WES: Otis. I'm not sure I ever heard the name!

HAYAAM: Do you know what he meant by it?

WES: Of course. Since the American colonies couldn't vote, they shouldn't be taxed.

HAYAAM: And what did he want to do about it?

WES: They went to war for their independence over it.

HAYAAM: But this is not what James Otis

meant when he said, "No taxation without representation." He meant, therefore the colonies should be represented in the English Parliament so they could vote. He didn't want war. When war came, he went crazy. They had to carry him out of Boston in a strait jacket.

Wes is amazed at how much she knows. This is all news to him. He can't think of anything to say.

> HAYAAM: You should read the history of your country. It is very fascinating.

INT. HARDING HOME - LIVING ROOM - DAY

Walter is reading. Evelyn is not in the room.

Wes and Hayaam enter.

> WES: We're done. Is mom around?

> WALTER: She sends her regrets. She's not feeling well.

> WES: What's the matter?

> WALTER: She's not sure. Maybe the flu coming on.

> HAYAAM: I'm very sorry.

> WALTER: Maybe next time. How did it go?

> WES: She knows American history better than I do.

Hayaam blushes.

EXT. HARDING HOME - DAY

Wes and Hayaam come out.

A car is parked out front, waiting for her. Wes is surprised to see it.

> HAYAAM: I told my brother to pick me up. He didn't want me to come. This is our compromise. He's afraid we're dating.

She studies Wes for a response. None comes.

> HAYAAM: Are we dating?

> WES: It's allowed?

> HAYAAM: If I choose to, yes. Remember, I am a feminist.

> WES: I keep forgetting.

> HAYAAM: Are we dating?

> WES: Well ... what do you think?

> HAYAAM: Please answer the question.

Wes takes a deep breath.

> WES: Yes. We're dating. I mean, I would like to think that we are.
>
> HAYAAM: Good. I like dating you.

She gives him a broad smile, turns and walks briskly to the car.

Wes watches her get in. The car speeds off.

INT. ABDUL'S CAR - DAY

Hayaam's smile is gone. She looks nervous, like she's waiting for something unpleasant.

> ABDUL-HAKEEM: Did you manage to get any studying done?
>
> HAYAAM: That's all we did. He asked questions from the book, and I gave the answers.
>
> ABDUL-HAKEEM: Seeing him will not lead to anything good.
>
> HAYAAM: This is my decision, not yours.
>
> ABDUL-HAKEEM: And papa's decision?
>
> HAYAAM: Papa is not here.
>
> ABDUL-HAKEEM: He will be here soon enough.

Hayaam's expression changes to expectation. She

waits for more.

> ABDUL-HAKEEM: He sent a letter. His papers are finally approved.
>
> HAYAAM: How soon will he leave?
>
> ABDUL-HAKEEM: Only a matter of weeks now.

Hayaam looks excited.

INT. HARDING HOME - MASTER BEDROOM - DAY

Wes stands at the door, which is cracked. He peeks in to see Evelyn lying on the bedspread.

> WES: Mom, are you okay?
>
> EVELYN: Oh Wesley ...

He steps into the room.

> WES: What's the matter?
>
> EVELYN: Why couldn't you get interested in an American girl?
>
> WES: She's studying to become an American.
>
> EVELYN: You know what I mean. She's a Muslim, isn't she? And you know nothing about her past.

WES: I know she's studying to become an American citizen.

EVELYN: She still belongs to the same religion as...

Evelyn can't finish.

EVELYN: What would your brother think?

WES: I can't believe you're saying this. It goes against everything Unitarians believe.

EVELYN: I'm a Baptist.

WES: What?

EVELYN: It's the only church I could get your father to go to. In my heart, I'm a Baptist.

EXT. NYC - PARK - DAY

Wes and Hayaam sit on a blanket in a park. He reads to her from "The Rubiyat."

WES: "Here with a Loaf of Bread beneath the Bough, / A Flask of Wine, a Book of Verse–and Thou / Beside me singing in the Wilderness– / And Wilderness is Paradise enow."

Hayaam takes the book.

She looks for a particular verse. And finds it.

> HAYAAM: "Ah, fill the Cup:—what boots it to repeat / How Time is slipping underneath our Feet: / Unborn tomorrow, and dead yesterday, / Why fret about them if TO-DAY be sweet!"

Their eyes are locked. It seems as if they might kiss.

Hayaam breaks it by holding out the book, returning it.

> WES: It's for you. You probably already have a copy.

> HAYAAM: I don't. Thank you. You must sign it.

Wes takes the book. He takes out a pen.

What to write?

> HAYAAM: Sign it, "from your life saver."

Wes almost blushes. He signs: "To Hayaam, whom I'll never forget, from your life saver, Wes."

He hands her the book. Hayaam is pleased with the inscription.

An awkward moment.

> HAYAAM: I'd better go home.

> WES: You're sure?
>
> HAYAAM: Yes.
>
> WES: You'll still come to church with me?

Now she looks straight at him.

> HAYAAM: Of course.

EXT. HARDING HOME - DAY

Wes comes out of the house. He is wearing a suit.

He gets into his car and heads out.

INT. HARDING HOME - LIVING ROOM - DAY

Evelyn comes into the room, dressed for church. Walter, in a suit, is waiting for her.

> EVELYN: Where's Wesley?
>
> WALTER: He said he'd meet us there.

Evelyn is puzzled by this but too much in a rush to say something.

EXT. UNITARIAN CHURCH - DAY

Congregants enter the church.

INT. UNITARIAN CHURCH - SANCTUARY -

DAY

Walter and Evelyn have taken their seats. Walter is saving room beside him, enough for two.

Evelyn scans the back of the room.

> EVELYN: It's not like him to be late.

Wes appears – with Hayaam. She is wearing her full Muslim garb, of course, in bright colors.

> EVELYN: *(to Walter, hushed panic)* My God, he brought her here!

Evelyn is tense as she waits.

Wes proudly walks down the aisle with Hayaam. She is quite the center of attention. The Unitarians seem happy to see her. Liberal smiles everywhere.

They reach the row where Walter has saved their seats.

> WES: Mother, this is Hayaam.

Evelyn puts on a good act.

> EVELYN: Oh, it's so wonderful to meet you at last.

> HAYAAM: It is a pleasure to meet you.

> WALTER: Let's scoot down for them, mother.

Walter and Evelyn make room, and Wes and Hayaam take their seats.

INT. UNITARIAN CHURCH - SANCTUARY - DAY (LATER)

The congregation is on its feet, singing a hymn.

Wes holds a hymnal for himself and Hayaam. She tries to follow along as best she can.

Evelyn glances their way. She tries to hide her concern.

EXT. UNITARIAN CHURCH - DAY

The minister, REV. SALLY DOWNS, is greeting the congregants as they exit.

Wes and Hayaam appear.

> WES: Rev. Downs, this is Hayaam.
>
> REV. SALLY DOWNS: Thank you so much for coming.
>
> WES: She's studying to become a citizen.
>
> REV. SALLY DOWNS: Well, this is an honor. I hope to see you again.
>
> HAYAAM: Thank you.

They move on.

Walter and Evelyn are next.

>REV. SALLY DOWNS: Thank you for bringing Hayaam.

Evelyn gives her a frozen smile.

EXT. UNITARIAN CHURCH - SIDEWALK - DAY

Walter and Evelyn join Wes and Hayaam.

>WALTER: Will you join us for lunch?

Wes looks at Hayaam for a clue.

>HAYAAM: I'm sorry. I must get home.

>WALTER: Some other time then.

INT. WES' CAR - DAY

Wes is driving, Hayaam beside him.

>HAYAAM: I said what you call "a white lie." I don't have to go home yet.

>WES: Why?

>HAYAAM: Your mother doesn't like me.

>WES: Of course she does.

He's not very convincing and sees that Hayaam

knows this.

> WES: My mother is, well ... she was raised a Baptist. They aren't very liberal minded about religious matters. But she's come a long way, believe me.
>
> HAYAAM: If she is a Baptist, why is she going to a Unitarian church?
>
> WES: Because my father wants to.

Hayaam smiles knowingly.

> WES: What?
>
> HAYAAM: American women are so repressed.

EXT. PARK - DAY

Wes and Hayaam stroll through a park.

They are silent but there is sense of growing togetherness. Several times each appears about to speak but stops. Finally ...

> WES: I have this great desire to hold your hand.
>
> HAYAAM: I would like that.

He takes her hand. They smile and continue on.

EXT. PARK - BENCH - DAY

They sit on a park bench.

> WES: Did you find church interesting?
>
> HAYAAM: Yes. I find all religions interesting. But I was surprised, too.
>
> WES: In what way?
>
> HAYAAM: I heard nothing about God or Jesus Christ. Even in the prayer, it was to the Great Spirit. I thought only your American Indians prayed to the Great Spirit.

Wes can't help himself and smiles.

> WES: Most unitarians are refugees from other religions. God and Christ sometimes bring bad memories of how they were brought up.
>
> HAYAAM: This is a strange foundation for a religion.
>
> WES: Well, it's not the official doctrine or anything.
>
> HAYAAM: Would you like to come to a mosque?
>
> WES: I would, yes.
>
> HAYAAM: When?

WES: Whenever would be appropriate.

HAYAAM: I don't know what this means. How would it be appropriate?

WES: Hayaam, I will come whenever you invite me.

HAYAAM: Today at sunset then.

INT. MOSQUE - DAY (SUNSET)

Lines of Muslims in prayer in a large spacious room.

Near the rear is a line of women. Hayaam stands behind Wes, who is in the first line of men in front of her.

Wes tries to follow along as best he can. An Arabic prayer is spoken. Everyone then gets to their knees. They lean forward, their foreheads touching the ground.

EXT. MOSQUE - NIGHT (EVENING)

Everyone comes out after prayer.

Wes looks very much out of place. He glances around for Hayaam.

Hayaam and Areebah come out together. Wes expectantly waits for them.

But they pass by him without Hayaam even acknowledging his presence.

Wes is stunned. He doesn't know what to do. Arab men are staring at him.

He moves off, following Hayaam and Areebah from a distance.

EXT. STREET - SIDEWALK - NIGHT (EVENING)

Wes follows the women, keeping about a quarter block between them. They continue down a sidewalk, away from the Mosque.

Suddenly Hayaam and Areebah stop. Wes stops.

Hayaam and Areebah exchange words, something Wes doesn't hear. Then Areebah walks away.

Hayaam looks at Wes, waiting.

Wes cautiously approaches.

> HAYAAM: I'm sorry. What I did will be controversial enough. I didn't want to cause a scene.
>
> WES: I wasn't supposed to be there?
>
> HAYAAM: A woman normally doesn't bring a male guest.
>
> WES: Will you get in trouble?

HAYAAM: I am used to being in trouble. Will you walk me home?

WES: Of course.

EXT. HAYAAM'S NEIGHBORHOOD - STREET - NIGHT (EVENING)

Wes and Hayaam approach Hayaam's apartment building. She stops.

HAYAAM: I'll say goodbye here.

WES: I feel like I got you in trouble.

HAYAAM: No more than I would be in anyway. Not everyone understands women like me, especially most Muslim men.

WES: How about your brother?

HAYAAM: Sometimes yes, sometimes no. Will I see you on campus tomorrow?

WES: I'd like that.

HAYAAM: Tea after my class?

WES: Great.

She smiles and moves off.

WES: *(after her)* Thank you!

She stops and turns, looking puzzled.

>WES: For taking me to the mosque. It was very educational.

She starts to say something but thinks against it. She smiles and continues on.

INT. HARDING HOME - DINING ROOM - NIGHT

The family at dinner.

>WES: I'd like to invite Hayaam for dinner.

Walter looks at Evelyn. She freezes.

>WALTER: Wes, it may be early for that.

>EVELYN: Why? He's determined to see her. Why will the situation be better later?

>WALTER: What I meant is, maybe you'll be able to accept her more graciously later.

>EVELYN: Graciously? Is that what I'm supposed to do?

She stands up.

>EVELYN: Those people killed my son. How can I be gracious about it.

>WES: Mother, you make it sound like she's a terrorist. She's becoming an American

citizen.

EVELYN: How wonderful for her.

She leaves the room.

WALTER: Wes, I don't think this is a good idea right now.

Wes doesn't respond. They continue eating silently.

INT. HAYAAM'S APARTMENT - BEDROOM - NIGHT

Hayaam is studying.

Abdul appears in the doorway. He knocks on the door frame.

Hayaam looks up.

HAYAAM: Come in.

ABDUL-HAKEEM: Tell me it isn't true.

HAYAAM: You want me to lie?

ABDUL-HAKEEM: Why?

HAYAAM: He is curious about Islam. He showed me his church, so I showed him mine.

ABDUL-HAKEEM: You know what father would say about this. He arrives next week.

Hayaam is caught between joy and apprehension.

> ABDUL-HAKEEM: He will tell you not to see this man. You know he will.
>
> HAYAAM: I know.

EXT. NYU CAMPUS - BASKETBALL COURT - DAY

Wes and Roger shooting baskets.

> ROGER: You still seeing the Arab lady?
>
> WES: She's from Indonesia.
>
> ROGER: I take it that's a yes.

Wes ignores the question. He shoots a basket.

> ROGER: Why?

Wes still ignores him.

> ROGER: I just don't get it.
>
> WES: I'm trying to feel like life is normal again. What's wrong with that?
>
> ROGER: Life will never be normal again.

Wes, not responding, shoots a basket.

A SERIES OF SHOTS

Wes and Hayaam continue to see one another.

– They have coffee and tea in the campus cafeteria.

– They window shop in a mall.

– They ride rental bikes through a park.

– They ride in a horse and carriage.

EXT. PARK - DAY

Wes tries to teach Hayaam how to throw a frisbee.

He demonstrates.

He hands the frisbee to Hayaam. She doesn't get a good trajectory on it.

He tries again. Failure again.

He hands her the frisbee. He stands behind her and reaches around to guide her through the motion of throwing.

And this is when he realizes what he is doing. He freezes.

They are practically embraced. The moment is charged with sexual energy.

Hayaam breaks it.

HAYAAM: Show me how.

Wes regains his composure. He guides her through the arm motion of throwing it.

> WES: Like this and let go ... this and let go ... try it.

He steps back. She throws. Much better.

EXT. PARK - DAY (LATER)

They are throwing the frisbee back and forth. Hayaam has the hang of it.

The trouble is, the physical exercise keeps displacing her head veil. Now and again it falls off her hair.

Frustrated, Hayaam lets the veil stay off. Wes sees her hair for the first time.

He holds the frisbee, not returning it. He approaches her.

Hayaam keeps the veil off her head.

He arrives. They stand close.

Wes reaches out and touches her hair.

> WES: You have beautiful hair.
>
> HAYAAM: I know.

> WES: I don't know why you cover it up.
>
> HAYAAM: It is my choice who sees it. No one else's.
>
> WES: I'm glad you let me see it.
>
> HAYAAM: So am I.

The sexual energy between them is greater than ever. Wes leans forward, slowly, an approach to kiss her.

At the last minute, Hayaam turns her head, offering her cheek. Wes kisses her cheek.

He pulls back. She moves forward. He prepares for a kiss on the lips but she kisses him on the cheek.

> HAYAAM: I have never kissed a man before.

EXT. HAYAAM'S APARTMENT - STREET - DAY

Wes walks Hayaam home.

INT. HAYAAM'S APARTMENT - DAY

Abdul watches them from a window.

EXT. HAYAAM'S APARTMENT - DAY

They stop in front of the house.

> WES: I want to kiss you again.

HAYAAM: I know. But not now, not here.

WES: I know.

HAYAAM: I'll see you tomorrow.

WES: You certainly will.

They exchange smiles. Wes turns and goes.

INT. HAYAAM'S APARTMENT - DAY

Through the window, Abdul sees Hayaam approaching.

He hurries away. He moves through the house and goes out the back door.

EXT. STREET - DAY

Wes is walking on the sidewalk when Abdul trots up and joins him.

> ABDUL-HAKEEM: You must stop seeing her.

> WES: I don't want to do that.

> ABDUL-HAKEEM: You must, for her own good.

> WES: She doesn't want to do that either.

> ABDUL-HAKEEM: Our father arrives in

this country next week. He is very traditional. You only cause family trouble.

WES: I get the impression Hayaam does exactly what she wants to do. If she wants to see me, she will.

ABDUL-HAKEEM: You are right. This is why I am asking you to do the honorable thing. Stop seeing her. Prevent our family from this trouble.

WES: I can't.

ABDUL-HAKEEM: Why do you do this? You think she will marry you? Even as radical as she is, she will only marry a Muslim. She will not sleep with a man before marriage. What is in this for you?

WES: I love her.

Abdul laughs.

ABDUL-HAKEEM: What do Americans know about love?

WES: I don't see any point in this conversation.

ABDUL-HAKEEM: Then I will tell you the point. I have asked you to do the honorable thing, to honor our family. If you betray this request, then you will pay the consequences.

> WES: Are you threatening me?
>
> ABDUL-HAKEEM: Stop seeing her.

He turns and leaves. Wes looks tense as he watches him go.

EXT. HARDING HOME - WES' ROOM - NIGHT

Wes is studying.

His father appears in the doorway.

> WALTER: Hayaam is here to see you.

Wes looks surprised. He stands.

> WALTER: Wes ... maybe you'd better talk to her outside.

EXT. HARDING HOME - PORCH - NIGHT

Wes and Hayaam sit on the porch.

> WES: I don't want to cause any problems for you. But I also want to keep seeing you.
>
> HAYAAM: I want to keep seeing you, too.
>
> WES: Abdul said your father will be angry.
>
> HAYAAM: Yes. He's been angry with me before.

WES: I feel like I'm between a rock and a hard place.

HAYAAM: What is this?

WES: A saying. I don't know what to do.

HAYAAM: Father will always love me. Even when he is mad.

WES: I think maybe you have to lead the way here. I don't want to force you to make your father angry.

HAYAAM: You think you can force me to do something?

Wes has to smile.

WES: Of course not. A slip of the tongue.

HAYAAM: Kiss me.

He leans forward and kisses her on the cheek.

HAYAAM: Not there.

She closes her eyes and puckers up. The moment has its comic element, which Wes recognizes. But he goes along, moving slowly forward.

A gentle kiss on the lips.

Hayaam opens her eyes. They are still very close, their lips almost touching.

HAYAAM: Again.

They kiss again, gently. And a third time, this time a tad more passionately. Hayaam is a quick study.

Hayaam throws her arms around him. They kiss even more passionately.

INT. HARDING HOME - NIGHT

Evelyn stands at a window, watching Wes and Hayamm kiss on the porch.

Walter appears behind her. He takes her arm. He leads her away.

EXT. HARDING HOME - PORCH - NIGHT

Wes and Hayaam finally stop kissing.

> HAYAAM: I will go now. No matter what happens, I will never forget tonight.
>
> WES: Neither will I.
>
> HAYAAM: I will see you on campus tomorrow.
>
> WES: Tomorrow's Saturday.
>
> HAYAAM: I am studying in the library. I will be done at one.
>
> WES: I'll be there.

HAYAAM: I never understood why you would want to do that before.

WES: Want to kiss?

HAYAAM: That, too. But the other.

WES: I'm not sure what you mean.

HAYAAM: To sleep with a man before you were married.

A question visibly on her mind, troubling her. Having said it, she rushes away.

Wes closes his eyes, treasuring the moment.

EXT. NEW YORK - AIRPORT - DAY

A jetliner lands.

INT. AIRPORT - PASSENGER TERMINAL - DAY

Hayaam and Abdul wait for the passengers to enter.

And here they come, walking in from the tunnel.

Hayaam searches the crowd for her father. So does Abdul.

Their father, JAMAL, 50s, appears in the flow of entering passengers. Abdul sees him first.

ABDUL-HAKEEM: Papa! Papa!

Now Hayaam sees him.

HAYAAM: Papa!

Jamal waves, smiling.

Suddenly two FBI AGENTS, dressed in suits, step in front of Jamal. They lead him off toward a door.

Hayaam and Abdul watch what is happening.

ABDUL-HAKEEM: Papa!

He starts toward them, with Hayaam in pursuit.

The agents reach the door. One opens it, and the other pushes Jamal inside.

The door closes. Abdul reaches it and starts pounding on the closed door. Hayaam arrives. Abdul keeps pounding on the door.

ABDUL-HAKEEM: Open the door! Papa!

An AIRPORT OFFICIAL hears the commotion and runs up.

AIRPORT OFFICIAL: What's the problem here?

ABDUL-HAKEEM: Some men took my father in there. I demand to know what is going on.

AIRPORT OFFICIAL: Come with me.

ABDUL-HAKEEM: I demand–!

HAYAAM: Abdul! Let's go with him. Please.

INT. AIRPORT - PRIVATE WAITING ROOM - DAY

Hayaam and Abdul sit, waiting. They are anxious.

An FBI man enters. Hayaam and Abdul quickly get to their feet.

FBI MAN: Your father is being detained for questioning.

ABDUL-HAKEEM: Questioning for what?

FBI MAN: That's all I know right now. You are free to go.

ABDUL-HAKEEM: I'm not leaving without my father.

FBI MAN: Unless you want to be detained yourself, I suggest you go.

ABDUL-HAKEEM: No!

HAYAAM: Abdul, we should go. We can't help father if you join him.

Abdul reluctantly gives in, and they leave.

INT. HARDING HOME - DINING ROOM - DAY

Walter is reading the morning paper when Wes passes through. Evelyn is nowhere to be seen.

> WALTER: Having breakfast?

> WES: Running late. See you tonight.

Wes hurries out.

Walter continues reading. A headline on the front page reads: "Suspected terrorist arrested at airport."

INT. NYU CAMPUS - COFFEE SHOP - DAY

Wes sits alone at a table. He looks at his watch.

INT. NYU CAMPUS - CLASSROOM - DAY

Wes comes into an empty classroom. He's too late.

EXT. NYU CAMPUS - PHONE BOOTH - DAY

Wes is on the phone. It rings and rings. He hangs up.

INT. HARDING HOME - WES' ROOM - NIGHT

Wes is on the phone, waiting for someone to answer.

ABDUL-HAKEEM: *(filtered)* Hello?

WES: May I speak to Hayaam, please?

ABDUL-HAKEEM: *(filtered)* Who is this?

Wes hesitates.

WES: It's Wes.

ABDUL-HAKEEM: *(filtered)* I told you to stop seeing her.

He hangs up.

Wes is stunned.

EXT. HAYAAM'S APARTMENT - NIGHT

Wes stands outside Hayaam's apartment. He looks through the lighted windows but fails to get a glimpse of her.

EXT. NYU CAMPUS - DAY

Wes walks across campus.

He sees a woman in Arab dress ahead. He rushes to her.

It's Areeba.

WES: Hi. Where's Hayaam?

Areeba looks around nervously.

> WES: What's the matter?

Areeba almost speaks but changes her mind.

> WES: What's going on? Tell me ... please.
>
> AREEBAH: Her father was arrested. They think he's a terrorist.

EXT. HARDING HOME - UTILITY PORCH - DAY

Wes goes through a stack of old newspapers.

He finds the one with the headline about Jamal's arrest. He starts reading.

EXT. NYC - BUSINESS AREA - DAY

Wes enters a skyscraper. He has the newspaper folded under his arm.

INT. SKYSCRAPER - OFFICE RECEPTION - DAY

Wes approaches a SECRETARY. She smiles as soon as she seems him.

> SECRETARY: Wesley! How nice to see you.
>
> WES: Is dad busy?
>
> SECRETARY: Go right in.

INT. WALTER'S OFFICE - DAY

Wes steps inside. Walter looks up from his desk.

> WALTER: This is a pleasant surprise.
>
> WES: Did you read this?

He shows his father the front page article about the arrest.

> WALTER: I did. A dangerous new world we live in.
>
> WES: This is Hayaam's father.
>
> WALTER: Are you sure?
>
> WES: Dad, he probably needs a lawyer.

Walter takes a deep breath.

> WALTER: Let's get some coffee.

INT. SKYSCRAPER - COFFEE SHOP - DAY

Wes and Walter sit at a table over coffee.

> WES: I know Hayaam. She doesn't come from a family of terrorists. Dad, please trust me on this.
>
> WALTER: How well do you know her? Or am I prying?

> WES: I like her a lot.

Walter studies him.

> WES: I know how complicated everything is. But that's another issue. Her father needs a lawyer, a damn good one under the circumstances. You've always been a champion of the underdog.
>
> WALTER: And what client would be more unpopular than this one?
>
> WES: Exactly.
>
> WALTER: I'll speak to him.
>
> WES: Thanks, Dad!

He reaches across the table and squeezes his father's hand.

EXT. HAYAAM'S APARTMENT - NIGHT

Wes again stands outside her apartment.

Then he catches a glimpse of her in a ground-floor window, her bedroom.

He moves quickly to the window. He looks inside.

Hayaam is preparing to study.

He taps on the window pane. Hayaam looks to the

window.

He taps lightly again.

Hayaam comes to the window and recognizes him. She looks behind her, quickly steps across the room and closes the bedroom door.

She hurries back and lifts open the window.

> HAYAAM: What are you doing here?
>
> WES: I heard about your father. I have to talk to you.
>
> HAYAAM: Meet me at the corner.

Wes darts way.

INT. HAYAAM'S APARTMENT - LIVING ROOM - NIGHT

Abdul is reading. Hayaam enters.

> HAYAAM: I'm going to the store. Do you need anything?
>
> ABDUL-HAKEEM: No.

EXT. HAYAAM'S NEIGHBORHOOD - CORNER - NIGHT

Wes waits for Hayaam. Then he sees her.

They spontaneously meet in an embrace.

Lost in the moment, Wes kisses her on the lips.

Hayaam doesn't resist for a moment. Then she breaks it.

> WES: I'm sorry ...
>
> HAYAAM: Don't apologize.
>
> WES: I read about your father. My dad's a lawyer, one of the best in the city. He'd like to talk to him. Maybe he'll represent him.
>
> HAYAAM: Your father would be his lawyer?
>
> WES: I think so. He has to talk to him first.
>
> HAYAAM: Why does he care?
>
> WES: He cares because I care.

This touches Hayaam. She moves back into his embrace.

EXT. NYC - FEDERAL BUILDING - DAY

A cab stops. Getting out are Walter, Wes and Hayaam. Walter carries a briefcase.

> WALTER: There's a coffee shop down the block. I'll meet you there in an hour.

INT. NYC - COFFEE SHOP - DAY

Wes and Hayaam enter.

Several customers stare at Hayaam. She looks self-conscious.

> WES: Want to take a walk?
>
> HAYAAM: Yes.

They leave.

INT. FEDERAL BUILDING - PRISONER VISITING AREA - DAY

Walter sits at a table, waiting.

A GUARD brings in Jamal. He legs and hands are shackled. The guard sits him down across from Walter and moves back.

> WALTER: I'm Walter Harding. I'm a lawyer.

Jamal stares at him.

> WALTER: My son told me about you. He's a friend of Hayaam's.
>
> JAMAL: Hayaam knows your son?

He doesn't look pleased at the prospect.

> WALTER: Yes. Do you know why you've been arrested?
>
> JAMAL: They say I am a terrorist. I am no

terrorist.

WALTER: That's a good place to start.

EXT. NYC - STREET - DAY

Wes and Hayaam walk.

>WES: Dad's a great lawyer. He'll do what's best, believe me.
>
>HAYAAM: Everything is different now. The way people look at me, wondering if I'm a terrorist.
>
>WES: That's not true.
>
>HAYAAM: I see how they look at me.
>
>WES: Only a few. You saw how welcome you were at my church.
>
>HAYAAM: I still don't understand why you call this a church if there is no mention of God.
>
>WES: We define God as spirit.
>
>HAYAAM: A God must be more than spirit.

EXT. NYC - FEDERAL BUILDING - DAY

Walter comes outside, carrying his briefcase.

INT. NYC - COFFEE SHOP - DAY

Walter enters. He looks around for Wes and Hayaam.

EXT. NYC - COFFEE SHOP - DAY

Walter comes back out just as Wes and Hayaam arrive.

> WES: How'd it go?
>
> WALTER: I'm going to represent him – at least until he finds a Muslim lawyer.
>
> WES: That's great.
>
> HAYAAM: How is he?
>
> WALTER: Under the circumstances, he's doing better than I expected.
>
> HAYAAM: What will happen now?
>
> WALTER: My first task is to make an argument for getting him out on bail.
>
> WES: Will this be a problem?
>
> WALTER: Given the climate, it could be.

EXT. NYC - PARK - DAY

Wes and Hayaam stroll through a park. They are holding hands.

EXT. PARK - ANOTHER AREA - DAY

Watching them through binoculars is Abdul. With him are OMAR and IMAD, both college age.

> ABDUL-HAKEEM: Here.

He hands the binoculars to Omar, who looks. Omar hands them to Imad, who looks.

> OMAR: You want us to get him now?

> ABDUL-HAKEEM: No. I will give my sister one more chance to stop seeing him. But I want you to stick to him like glue.

Abdul breaks into laughter.

> ABDUL-HAKEEM: Isn't this a wonderful expression? Stick to him like glue!

EXT. PARK - WALKWAY - DAY

Wes and Hayaam still hold hands.

> WES: Will you come to church with me Sunday?

> HAYAAM: Are you trying to convert me?

> WES: No! I just want you to see that you have friends here.

She pulls away her hand.

> HAYAAM: This becomes very complicated.
>
> WES: It doesn't have to be. Does it?
>
> HAYAAM: What is our future?
>
> WES: I don't know. I'm too busy thinking about now, the present tense. I know I want to spend as much of it as possible with you.
>
> HAYAAM: Yes, I know the feeling.
>
> WES: This can't be bad, can it?
>
> HAYAAM: I don't know what it is. It's too new to me.

Wes makes a move to kiss her.

> HAYAAM: No. I think I should go home.

EXT. NYC - STREET - DAY

Wes hails a cab for Hayaam. It swerves to the curb.

> HAYAAM: Thank you for everything.
>
> WES: See you at school tomorrow?
>
> HAYAAM: Yes.

She smiles, though there is a touch of sadness in it. She gets into the cab.

Wes hands the cabbie some money. He steps back and watches the cab pull away. Then he starts down the street.

Some distance behind, Omar and Imad follow him.

INT. NYC - BAR - DAY

Wes enters a bar. He takes a stool.

EXT. NYC - BAR - DAY

Omar and Imad stand outside the bar. They look confused about entering or not.

INT. NYC - BAR - DAY

Wes sips a beer.

Omar and Imad enter. They sit down the bar from Wes.

Farther down the bar, a DRUNK CUSTOMER sees them take stools.

> DRUNK CUSTOMER: Since when is this a watering hole for fucking A-rabs?

The BARTENDER rushes forward, a reluctant peace-maker.

> BARTENDER: Hold you tongue, Charlie. *(to Omar and Imad)* I gotta serve you, but you might want to think about it. Charlie's got a bad temper.

Omar and Imad exchange a glance.

> WES: You go to NYU? I think I've seen you on campus.
>
> OMAR: Yes.
>
> WES: Can I buy you a beer?

This takes them completely aback. Imad stands up.

> IMAD: We don't want to cause trouble.

He gestures to Omar to leave.

> WES: Get them two beers.
>
> OMAR: No, please. Thank you very much.

Omar and Imad get the hell out of there.

The bartender comes over and stares at Wes.

> BARTENDER: Aren't you something.

Wes gulps down his beer and stands.

> BARTENDER: You got something to say to me?
>
> WES: No, sir, I don't.

EXT. NYC - BAR - DAY

Omar and Imad, looking through the window, see Wes coming for the door. They hurry down the street and duck into a doorway.

Wes comes out and heads up the sidewalk.

Omar and Imad follow him.

INT. HARDING HOME - DINING ROOM - NIGHT

The family at dinner.

> WES: How's the argument for bail coming, Dad?
>
> WALTER: Ask me in a few days.

Evelyn glares at Walter. He notices it.

> WALTER: Evelyn, don't.
>
> EVELYN: I don't understand why you're doing this.
>
> WALTER: Even if he's guilty, he deserves a lawyer.
>
> EVELYN: Does it have to be you?

They eat on in silence.

INT. NYU CAMPUS - COFFEE SHOP - DAY

Wes and Hayaam having coffee. They hold hands

across the table.

Across the room sit Abdul, Omar and Imad, watching them.

Hayaam looks at her watch.

> HAYAAM: I don't want to be late.
>
> WES: You're sure you don't want me to go with you.
>
> HAYAAM: This is something I must do myself.

Hayaam gets up. Wes gets up to embrace her. Then Hayaam walks away.

> WES: *(after her)* Good luck!

Hayaam waves.

Abdul watches her go.

> ABDUL-HAKEEM: Stay here.

Abdul leaves after Hayaam.

Omar and Imad stay at the table. They watch Wes, who sits back down.

EXT. NYU CAMPUS - DAY

Abdul catches up with Hayaam as she walks across campus.

ABDUL-HAKEEM: You are still seeing him.

HAYAAM: Are you spying on me?

ABDUL-HAKEEM: I'm a terrorist. That's what we do, spy on people.

She ignores the remark.

ABDUL-HAKEEM: You will break father's heart when he learns this.

HAYAAM: His father is helping us.

ABDUL-HAKEEM: We don't need his help.

HAYAAM: Of course we do. He's a very important lawyer.

ABDUL-HAKEEM: I'm asking you again, stop seeing him.

HAYAAM: I will not stop seeing him.

ABDUL-HAKEEM: Don't say I didn't warn you.

HAYAAM: What is that supposed to mean?

ABDUL-HAKEEM: How can you break father's heart? Especially now, with what he is going through.

HAYAAM: I'm in a hurry. I have my citizenship exam.

She walks on alone.

INT. NYU CAMPUS - COFFEE SHOP - DAY

Abdul returns to the table. Omar and Imad are still watching Wes.

> ABDUL-HAKEEM: Tonight.

Omar and Imad nod.

INT. FEDERAL BUILDING - TESTING ROOM - DAY

Hayaam takes her test. She looks pensive but is moving right along, answering multiple choice questions.

INT. HARDING HOME - WES' ROOM - NIGHT

Wes on phone, waiting for someone to answer. Nothing. He hangs up.

INT. HARDING HOME - LIVING ROOM - NIGHT

Walter reads the newspaper. Evelyn files her nails.

Wes comes into the room.

> WES: Anyone need anything at the store?

EVELYN: Are we out of half-and-half?

WES: I'll look. Dad?

Walter doesn't look up.

WALTER: Fine.

INT. HARDING HOME - KITCHEN - NIGHT

Wes looks into the refrigerator.

WES: *(calling to mother)* I'll get half-and-half!

EXT. HARDING HOME - NIGHT

Wes comes out. He heads up the street, a pleasant night for a walk.

Across the street Omar and Imad come out of the shadows.

EXT. HARDING NEIGHBORHOOD - STREET - NIGHT

Wes walks along at a brisk gait.

Omar and Imad are behind him.

EXT. CONVENIENCE MARKET - NIGHT

Wes enters the market.

Omar and Imad wait outside, a short distance away.

INT. CONVENIENCE MARKET - NIGHT

At the counter Wes buys half-and-half and a six-pack of pop.

EXT. HARDING NEIGHBORHOOD - STREET - NIGHT

Wes on his way home.

He passes a line of bushes. Suddenly Omar and Imad come from nowhere, jumping him.

They quickly knock him down. They start kicking him in the face and ribs.

Wes tries to defend himself with his arms. He's not doing a good job of it.

Omar and Imad keep kicking him.

A car turns onto the street, its headlights catching Wes on the ground.

Omar and Imad immediately flee.

The car stops and the DRIVER hurries out.

>	DRIVER: *(after Omar and Imad)* Hey!

He stoops to Wes on the ground.

EXT. HOSPITAL - NIGHT

An ambulance pulls into a hospital.

INT. HARDING HOME - KITCHEN - NIGHT

Evelyn is putting away dishes when the phone rings.

> EVELYN: Hello?

INT. HOSPITAL - HALLWAY - NIGHT

Walter and Evelyn hurry down a hallway at the hospital.

INT. HOSPITAL - WES' ROOM - NIGHT

They enter Wes' private room.

Wes is in bed. His face is black-and-blue, one eye swollen shut. His ribs are wrapped.

> EVELYN: Oh my God ...
>
> WES: You should see the other guy.

The joke falls flat.

INT. HOSPITAL - PARKING GARAGE - NIGHT

Walter and Evelyn step out of an elevator into a parking garage.

> EVELYN: See where it all leads? Will you stop now?

> WALTER: Pardon me?

> EVELYN: Representing that man. Wes seeing that girl. Look what comes of it.

> WALTER: I won't dignify that with a response.

The ice gets thick between them.

EXT. NYU CAMPUS - DAY

Students cross campus between classes.

One of them is Hayaam.

Areebah joins her.

> AREEBAH: Well?

> HAYAAM: I passed!

She is all smiles.

INT. NYU CAMPUS - COFFEE SHOP - DAY

She enters the coffee shop. She looks around for Wes but can't find him.

INT. NYU CAMPUS - ART STUDIO - DAY

Hayaam looks for Wes in his art studio.

INT. NYU CAMPUS - LIBRARY - DAY

Hayaam enters the area where Wes often studies. He isn't there.

EXT. HOSPITAL - DAY

Walter enters the hospital.

INT. HOSPITAL - WES' ROOM - DAY

Wes is sitting up in bed when Walter enters.

>WALTER: How are we feeling today?
>
>WES: I'm good. How are you?
>
>WALTER: Busy. And challenged. It's not looking good for Hayaam's father.
>
>WES: Has she called?
>
>WALTER: You'd have to ask your mother.
>
>WES: Where is she?
>
>WALTER: She'll come by tonight. She thinks we asked for all this. You seeing Hayaam, me helping her father.
>
>WES: She may be right.
>
>WALTER: Not you, too.
>
>WES: Hayaam's brother warned me not to

keep seeing her.

WALTER: You think he was behind this?

WES: I don't know. I'd like to talk to Hayaam. She probably doesn't even know I'm here.

WALTER: I was going to call and update her on the situation. I'll let her know.

WES: Thanks, Dad.

INT. HAYAAM'S APARTMENT - DAY

Hayaam is on the phone.

HAYAAM: Thank you, Mr. Harding. Please tell Wes I'll see him tonight. ... Goodbye.

She hangs up the phone. She looks furious.

INT. HAYAAM'S APARTMENT - ABDUL'S ROOM - DAY

Abdul is reading. Hayaam barges in.

HAYAAM: How could you!

ABDUL-HAKEEM: How could I what?

HAYAAM: You have no right to interfere in my life this way!

She storms out.

> ABDUL-HAKEEM: *(after her)* You have no right to destroy our family!

INT. HOSPITAL - WES' ROOM - NIGHT

Hayaam starts to enter just as a NURSE exits.

> HAYAAM: Is he all right?

The nurse is visibly uncomfortable with Hayaam, who as usual is in her traditional hijab.

> NURSE: Are you family?
>
> HAYAAM: Do I look like family?

The nurse glares at her.

> HAYAAM: I'm a friend.
>
> WES: *(O.S.)* Hayaam, is that you? Come on in.

Hayaam's turn to glare – and she steps into the room.

She clearly is shocked by his appearance.

> WES: I look worse than I feel, believe me. They're sending me home soon.
>
> HAYAAM: I'm so sorry. I feel like it's my fault.

> WES: Don't be ridiculous. Sit down, please.

She takes a chair near the bed.

EXT. HOSPITAL - PARKING GARAGE - NIGHT

Evelyn gets out of her car and heads for the elevator.

INT. HOSPITAL - WES' ROOM - NIGHT

Wes and Hayaam continue.

> WES: How did you do on your exam?
>
> HAYAAM: I passed it.
>
> WES: Fantastic. What's next?
>
> HAYAAM: I take my oath as a citizen.

INT. HOSPITAL - HALLWAY - NIGHT

Evelyn comes down the hallway, looking for a room. A nurse appears.

> NURSE: May I help you find someone?
>
> EVELYN: Wesley Harding.

INT. HOSPITAL - WES' ROOM - NIGHT

Wes and Hayaam are holding hands, silent a moment.

Evelyn appears in the doorway. No one sees her.

She's shocked by what she sees. She steps back, out of sight.

INT. HOSPITAL - HALLWAY - NIGHT

Outside her son's room, Evelyn has a hard time controlling her emotions. She rushes down the hallway to get away.

INT. HOSPITAL - PARKING GARAGE - NIGHT

Evelyn heads for her car when she meets Roger coming the other way.

> ROGER: Hi, Mrs. Harding. How's he doing today?
>
> EVELYN: That girl's with him.

She hurries on. Roger is dumbfounded, not sure what to say.

INT. HOSPITAL - WES' ROOM - NIGHT

Wes and Hayaam are still holding hands when Roger enters.

> ROGER: Knock, knock.
>
> WES: Hey! Good to see you.

ROGER: Man, you don't look ready for one-on-one at all.

WES: Give me a few days.

ROGER: Weeks, I'd say.

Hayaam stands up.

HAYAAM: I will leave now.

WES: I'm sorry. Roger, this is Hayaam. *(to Hayaam)* Roger.

HAYAAM: Hello.

ROGER: Nice to meet you.

HAYAAM: *(to Wes)* I'll see you again soon.

She leaves.

ROGER: Your mom looked upset.

WES: She was here?

ROGER: I ran into her in the parking garage.

INT. HARDING HOME - WALTER'S OFFICE - NIGHT

Walter is working at his desk.

Evelyn enters. Walter looks up.

WALTER: How's he doing?

EVELYN: That girl was there.

WALTER: And...?

EVELYN: They were holding hands. I didn't stay.

WALTER: Evelyn, you're going to have to learn how to accept this. I think he's very interested in her.

EVELYN: How can he ... ?

She can't finish.

WALTER: You can't wrap everyone in the same blanket just because they're from the Middle East.

EVELYN: I know that in theory. I suppose I do. But I lost my son, Walter.

WALTER: My son, too.

EVELYN: The country will never be the same again. I don't see how you can represent one of them.

WALTER: I'm a lawyer. Even if he were guilty–

EVELYN: I know the speech. I'm sorry. I

just don't know how to get closure. I'm going to bed.

She leaves.

Walter takes a deep breath, then goes back to work.

INT. HOSPITAL - WES' ROOM - DAY

Wes sits on the edge of the bed. A NURSE watches him.

Wes gets to his feet. He keeps his balance.

> NURSE: Very good.

Wes takes a step forward. Then another.

> NURSE: You're doing great.

Wes slowly walks across the room.

EXT. NYU CAMPUS - STUDENT UNION - DAY

Hayaam enters the Student Union building.

INT. NYU CAMPUS - COFFEE SHOP - DAY

She takes a cup of tea to a table and sits down.

She takes out the "Rubiyat" and begins reading from it.

Across the way sit Abdul, Omar and Imad.

ABDUL-HAKEEM: Excuse me.

Abdul joins Hayaam at her table.

ABDUL-HAKEEM: I found a lawyer for father.

HAYAAM: He has a lawyer.

ABDUL-HAKEEM: A Muslim. He's Pakistani.

HAYAAM: Wes' father is doing this for nothing.

ABDUL-HAKEEM: So will he. He's Muslim, he knows what we are going through now.

HAYAAM: Mr. Harding has a very good reputation.

ABDUL-HAKEEM: It's up to father. I'm giving him a choice.

Hayaam doesn't reply. She looks away.

ABDUL-HAKEEM: You saw him in the hospital, didn't you?

HAYAAM: And if I did?

ABDUL-HAKEEM: Why do you persist in doing this? The longer you see him, the worse everything will turn out.

Hayaam gathers her things to leave.

> ABDUL-HAKEEM: You aren't as stupid as you act. You know what you're doing has no future.

Hayaam hurries away.

INT. HOSPITAL - COUNTER - DAY

Wes stands at a counter, signing papers. Walter and Evelyn wait nearby.

Wes is done. He turns to his parents. He has a walking cane.

> WES: Ready.

EXT. HOSPITAL - DAY

Wes, Walter and Evelyn come out of the hospital. Wes moves one careful step at a time, the parents slowing down to stay with him.

Evelyn's car is parked nearby.

> WALTER: I'll see you two tonight.

He gives his son an awkward hug and moves off.

Evelyn opens the door for Wes.

INT. EVELYN'S CAR - DAY

Evelyn is driving.

> WES: It's nothing serious, mom.
>
> EVELYN: What?
>
> WES: Between Hayaam and me. Relax about it.

Evelyn forces a smile and drives on.

EXT. FEDERAL BUILDING - DAY

Walter enters the building.

INT. FEDERAL BUILDING - PRISONER VISITING AREA - DAY

Walter approaches the check-in desk. An OFFICER of the court is there.

> WALTER: Hello again.
>
> OFFICER: He's not here.
>
> WALTER: I beg your pardon?
>
> OFFICER: He was released last night.

INT. HAYAAM'S APARTMENT - DAY

Abdul embraces his father, Jamal. They stand just inside the front doorway.

> ABDUL-HAKEEM: I was so worried about

you.

>JAMAL: Where is Hayaam?

>ABDUL-HAKEEM: He's at the University until this afternoon.

>JAMAL: How is she?

Abdul hesitates.

>JAMAL: What is it? What is wrong?

>ABDUL-HAKEEM: Nothing is wrong. You are free!

INT. NYU CAMPUS - COFFEE SHOP - DAY

Hayaam sits at a table with Areebah. They speak in hushed tones.

>AREEBAH: I haven't told you what I think. But I worry about you.

>HAYAAM: Not you, too.

>AREEBAH: We are so different from people here. Especially now. I have to tell you, I'm thinking of going home.

>HAYAAM: Before you graduate?

>AREEBAH: Yes. I can get my degree in Jakarta.

HAYAAM: But to get an American degree, it's so prestigious. If you took this home, you could do anything.

AREEBAH: I've never been comfortable here. Now, of course, it is so much worse.

HAYAAM: Your parents wrote you, didn't they? They asked you to come home.

AREEBAH: They are right.

Hayaam looks around. Tables are crowded with American students, ignoring them.

HAYAAM: They get used to us.

AREEBAH: Not everyone. The people who beat up your friend – don't you think there are Americans who would do the same to you?

HAYAAM: I've not met these Americans. Tomorrow I will be an American myself.

AREEBAH: Hayaam, you are so naive.

Hayaam looks away. She looks worried.

EXT. HAYAAM'S APARTMENT - DAY

Hayaam approaches the house.

INT. HAYAAM'S APARTMENT - DAY

Hayaam comes inside. She takes off her back pack before she sees her father standing nearby. She screams for joy and rushes into his arms.

INT. HARDING HOME - DINING ROOM - NIGHT

Wes, Walter and Evelyn at dinner.

Evelyn gets up.

> EVELYN: I bought an apple pie from Rose's. Who wants ice cream on it?
>
> WES: I do.
>
> WALTER: Two.

She goes into the kitchen.

> WALTER: Her father was released last night. Apparently all charges were dropped.
>
> WES: Fantastic. Thanks, Dad.
>
> WALTER: Actually I hadn't even filed yet. I didn't do a thing.
>
> WES: Your reputation probably scared them.
>
> WALTER: I won't flatter myself.

INT. HARDING HOME - WES' ROOM - NIGHT

Wes is reading. He stops and goes to the phone.

He dials a number.

INT. HAYAAM'S APARTMENT - KITCHEN - NIGHT

Hayaam is putting away dishes when the phone rings.

> HAYAAM: I'll get it!

She picks up the receiver.

INTERCUT

> HAYAAM: Hello?

> WES: Hi. It's me.

Hayaam lowers her voice.

> HAYAAM: How are you?

> WES: I'm home.

> HAYAAM: I'm glad.

> WES: I want to see you.

Abdul walks into the kitchen.

HAYAAM: I'll see you at school tomorrow, okay?

WES: Sure.

HAYAAM: Goodnight.

She abruptly hangs up.

HAYAAM: *(to Abdul)* Areebah needed an assignment.

Abdul regards her suspiciously. Hayaam goes back to putting away dishes.

INT. HARDING HOME - WES' ROOM - NIGHT

Wes sits with the dead phone in his hand. He lowers it into the cradle.

EXT. HARDING HOME - DAY

Early morning. Walter comes out and fetches the morning paper.

EXT. HAYAAM'S APARTMENT - DAY

Early morning. Abdul comes out and gets the paper.

INT. HAYAAM'S APARTMENT - DINING ROOM - DAY

Jamal sits at the table. Abdul joins him with the

paper.

>JAMAL: Abdul, I've been thinking. How are you treated here?

>ABDUL-HAKEEM: How do you mean?

>JAMAL: In this place where they arrest an innocent man. Do you feel like a free man here?

>ABDUL-HAKEEM: I have learned to look over my shoulder. Especially now.

>JAMAL: That's what I mean. I could not sleep last night. I kept waiting for a knock on the door, the police have changed their mind, they haul me away into the night.

>ABDUL-HAKEEM: Father, what is it?

>JAMAL: I'm going home. I should never have come.

>ABDUL-HAKEEM: Then I will come with you.

>JAMAL: That's what I prayed for you to say. And Hayaam must come, too.

Abdul doesn't reply.

>JAMAL: She is so adventurous. Does she like it here?

ABDUL-HAKEEM: She feels the same hatred, I am sure.

JAMAL: Good. Will you tell her we are going home?

ABDUL-HAKEEM: Of course. When?

JAMAL: As soon as possible. Is there a problem?

ABDUL-HAKEEM: No. I will tell her today.

INT. NYU CAMPUS - ART STUDIO - DAY

Wes is working on his abstract of bright colors. It isn't going well.

Suddenly he paints black streaks over it. An act of destruction.

INT. NYU CAMPUS - COFFEE SHOP - DAY

Wes enters the coffee shop. He looks around. No Hayaam.

INT. NYU CAMPUS - CLASSROOM - DAY

Wes sits in class, listening to a lecture.

He stares out the window, lost in private thoughts.

INT. NYU CAMPUS - COFFEE SHOP - DAY

Wes comes into the coffee shop again. He sees Areebah sitting alone.

He goes to her table.

> WES: Have you seen Hayaam?
>
> AREEBAH: She wasn't in class today.
>
> WES: Is she ill?
>
> AREEBAH: Her father's home.
>
> WES: I heard. Great news.

Something in Areebah's expression alerts him.

> WES: What is it?
>
> AREEBAH: They are returning to Indonesia.

Wes is shocked to hear this.

> WES: When?
>
> AREEBAH: Right away.

EXT. NYU CAMPUS - PAY PHONE - DAY

Wes stands at a pay phone, waiting for an answer. Nothing.

EXT. NYC - "GROUND ZERO" - DAY

Wes strolls along the outskirts of Ground Zero. The long cleanup process continues.

He is lost in his thoughts.

INT. FEDERAL BUILDING - TESTING ROOM - DAY

Hayaam, with a group of other immigrants, all take an allegiance to the United States.

EXT. NYC - "GROUND ZERO" - DAY

Wes sketches the scene in a small artist's notebook.

EXT. FEDERAL BUILDING - DAY

Hayaam comes out. She is carrying a small American flag.

Abdul is waiting for her.

> ABDUL-HAKEEM: Areebah told me you would be here.
>
> HAYAAM: I'm an American.
>
> ABDUL-HAKEEM: Father wants to go home.
>
> HAYAAM: Home?
>
> ABDUL-HAKEEM: Back to Jakarta. All of us.

> HAYAAM: Why?
>
> ABDUL-HAKEEM: You have to ask? They treated him like a terrorist. He wants nothing to do with a country like this. I'm going home with him, and I think you should as well.
>
> HAYAAM: I'm in school.
>
> ABDUL-HAKEEM: So am I. We both can continue in Jakarta.

Hayaam is speechless.

> ABDUL-HAKEEM: If you are not going, you have to tell father yourself.

INT. HAYAAM'S APARTMENT - LIVING ROOM - DAY

Jamal is reading. Hayaam enters.

Jamal sees her and lights up.

> JAMAL: Hayaam. You look more like your mother every day.
>
> HAYAAM: Father, I must tell you something. I became an American citizen today.

Jamal looks surprised.

> JAMAL: I had no idea.

HAYAAM: I wrote you about it.

JAMAL: That was last year. I thought it was a passing fancy.

HAYAAM: I took the oath today.

JAMAL: What does this mean?

HAYAAM: I have the rights of an American citizen.

JAMAL: But you are born in Jakarta. This is your home.

HAYAAM: I am a citizen of both countries now.

JAMAL: And you want to live here?

HAYAAM: I'm sorry what they did to you.

JAMAL: It is the greatest humiliation of my life.

HAYAAM: I understand. The Americans, after what happened, they are not always thinking clearly before they act.

JAMAL: I cannot stay here.

HAYAAM: I understand.

JAMAL: I want us all to go home.

> HAYAAM: I have two homes now.
>
> JAMAL: No, this is not true. Not yet.
>
> HAYAAM: Father ...
>
> JAMAL: What would your mother say?

Hayaam looks off.

> JAMAL: Look at me. Tell me you will not return home. Tell me you will break up our family.

Hayaam thinks before replying, softly.

> HAYAAM: You know I can't do this.

INT. HARDING HOME - DINING ROOM - NIGHT

Evelyn enters carrying a casserole. Only Walter sits at the table.

> EVELYN: Where's Wesley?
>
> WALTER: I haven't seen him.

EXT. HAYAAM'S APARTMENT - NIGHT

Wes stands outside Hayaam's apartment. Lights are on, movement inside, but no glimpse of her.

Wes slowly approaches the house.

INT. HAYAAM'S APARTMENT - HAYAAM'S ROOM - NIGHT

Hayaam has clothes spread everywhere. She is trying to pack but not doing a very good job of it.

She hears something at the window. She turns.

Waits, listens. Nothing.

EXT. HAYAAM'S APARTMENT - HAYAAM'S ROOM (WINDOW) - NIGHT

Wes picks up a pebble and throws it against the window.

This time Hayaam comes forward – and sees him. She lifts open the window.

> WES: Areebah told me you are leaving.

> HAYAAM: Wait a minute.

INT. HAYAAM'S APARTMENT - HAYAAM'S ROOM - NIGHT

Hayaam looks around, grabs a jacket. She goes to the window and opens it wider.

EXT. HAYAAM'S APARTMENT - HAYAAM'S ROOM (WINDOW) - NIGHT

Wes helps her come out the window.

They embrace.

>HAYAAM: Where can we go?

>WES: I don't know.

>HAYAAM: Anywhere but here.

EXT. NYC - NEIGHBORHOOD STREET - NIGHT

They walk, holding hands. No one speaks.

EXT. NYC - COFFEE SHOP - NIGHT

They sit at a booth in a coffee shop. Wes has coffee, Hayaam tea.

>HAYAAM: I could not say no to him. Once he is settled again, I will come back. I want to live in America.

>WES: I'll wait for you.

>HAYAAM: Please don't say this.

>WES: I mean it.

>HAYAAM: We don't know what the future brings.

>WES: Hayaam, I love you.

This almost brings her to tears. She looks away.

She regains her composure and looks back to him.

> HAYAAM: In my country, a bride is expected to be a virgin. I have never questioned this before.

She stops, as if waiting for Wes to say something.

> WES: I'm not sure what to say.
>
> HAYAAM: This is something that only happens once, with only one man. You understand what I am saying?
>
> WES: I don't think so.
>
> HAYAAM: I want this man to be you.

Wes reaches across the table and takes her hand.

> WES: You're sure?
>
> HAYAAM: Yes. Tonight.

Wes is speechless.

> HAYAAM: We are leaving tomorrow.
>
> WES: But your classes ... ?
>
> HAYAAM: When father makes up his mind, there is no waiting. So we must do this tonight. Unless you don't want me.
>
> WES: Of course I want you.

> HAYAAM: Then you are in charge. I have no such experience.
>
> WES: I don't have all that much myself.
>
> HAYAAM: You don't know what to do?
>
> WES: I know what to do.

EXT. NYC - HOTEL - NIGHT

Wes and Hayaam stop outside a hotel.

> WES: Let me do all the talking.
>
> HAYAAM: I would have no idea what to say.

They enter.

INT. NYC - HOTEL - FRONT DESK - NIGHT

Wes approaches the front desk. Hayaam waits behind.

> WES: A double for my wife and I, please.
>
> DESK CLERK: Certainly, sir.

He glances quickly at Hayaam, then gets down to business.

INT. HOTEL - HALLWAY - NIGHT

An elevator door opens. Hayaam steps out first,

then Wes.

Wes looks at a sign on the wall.

> WES: This way.

INT. HOTEL - ROOM - NIGHT

They come into their hotel room. A small, clean room with a large King-sized bed.

Hayaam giggles nervously.

> WES: What's wrong?
>
> HAYAAM: I've never seen a bed this large.

Wes walks to a table where there's information on the hotel.

> WES: They have room service. Are you hungry?
>
> HAYAAM: A little, yes.
>
> WES: Do you drink champagne?
>
> HAYAAM: Not normally. Tonight, I think so.
>
> WES: Are you going to sit down?
>
> HAYAAM: Of course.

She sits on the edge of the bed.

WES: Here's the menu.

He brings it to her.

INT. HAYAAM'S APARTMENT - HAYAAM'S ROOM - NIGHT

Abdul steps into the doorway of Hayaam's room. He immediately sees the open window. He rushes to it.

INT. HOTEL - ROOM - NIGHT

Wes and Hayaam sit at a table over dinner. They're also sharing a bottle of champagne.

Hayaam sips.

> HAYAAM: I like this.
>
> WES: It can sneak up on you.
>
> HAYAAM: What does this mean?
>
> WES: You can feel tipsy without getting any warning that it's coming.
>
> HAYAAM: Then I will have a new experience!

She sips some more.

INT. HOSPITAL - ROOM - NIGHT (LATER)

Hayaam is on her feet. Her shoes are off. Her hijab is off, revealing a modest dress.

She is doing some kind of dance, on the ballet side.

Wes sits watching, grinning.

On the table, the champagne bottle is empty. The dinner plates are gone.

Hayaam loses her balance and steers herself to fall on the bed. Then she gets up and does a quick curtsy.

Wes applauds.

> HAYAAM: I am very ... what is it, tipsy?
>
> WES: Tipsy, indeed.
>
> HAYAAM: How long does it last?
>
> WES: Probably until you go to bed.
>
> HAYAAM: Maybe we should get some more champagne.
>
> WES: Maybe we should take a walk.
>
> HAYAAM: Yes! What a good idea. Where are my shoes?

EXT. HOTEL - NIGHT

Wes and Hayaam enter the night. The street is

quiet. It is late.

> HAYAAM: Where shall we go?
>
> WES: Maybe just walk a while.

They start off. Hayaam steadies herself against Wes, leaning against him.

EXT. NYC - STREET - NIGHT

They walk along. Hayaam still leans close against Wes. They move along together like lovers.

EXT. NYC - "GROUND ZERO" - NIGHT

Suddenly they are within sight of Ground Zero. Even from this distance, activity is in full force as men go through the rubble, cleaning up.

Hayaam sees what is ahead and stops.

> HAYAAM: Why did we come here?
>
> WES: I'm sorry. I wasn't paying attention where we were going. We can go back.
>
> HAYAAM: Not yet.

She takes his hand and leads the way closer to Ground Zero.

They come to a fence and stop.

> HAYAAM: My father says he was never so

humiliated.

> WES: I'm so sorry that happened. At least they let him go.
>
> HAYAAM: They had to. He was innocent.

Wes doesn't comment.

> HAYAAM: You understand why I have to go back, don't you?
>
> WES: Yes.

He doesn't sound convincing.

> HAYAAM: I will continue school in Jakarta. Then in two years, I will come to America for graduate school.
>
> WES: What will you study?
>
> HAYAAM: I used to think Philosophy. Maybe I will change my mind. Maybe I will become a translator at the United Nations.

They are silent a moment.

> HAYAAM: People from many nations died here. People from Indonesia, too. Not just Americans.
>
> WES: I know.
>
> HAYAAM: Some Americans forget this, I

think. They think they are the only ones who suffer.

WES: A minority, I think.

A silence.

WES: Shall we head back?

HAYAAM: Yes. I haven't forgotten.

WES: That's not what I meant.

HAYAAM: But it's what I meant.

INT. HOTEL - BATHROOM - NIGHT

Wes is brushing his teeth. He finishes.

INT. HOTEL - ROOM - NIGHT

He comes into the room in his shorts.

In bed, Hayaam is asleep, wearing bra and panties.

Wes crawls in beside her. He studies her.

He reaches over her to turn out the light.

EXT. HOTEL - LOBBY - DAY

Wes buys a newspaper.

He steps to the elevator and presses the button.

EXT. HOTEL - HALLWAY - DAY

Wes lets himself into the room.

INT. HOTEL - ROOM - DAY

Wes enters. The bed is empty. The bathroom door is closed.

INT. HOTEL - BATHROOM - DAY

Hayaam is in the shower.

INT. HOTEL - ROOM - DAY

Wes is reading the paper when Hayaam enters from the bathroom. She is dressed.

> WES: Good morning. How do you feel?
>
> HAYAAM: Terrible. Why do people drink if this is how they feel?
>
> WES: They like how they feel when they're drinking. We'll get you an aspirin in the restaurant.

INT. HOTEL - RESTAURANT - DAY

Wes and Hayaam over breakfast. Hayaam only picks at her food.

> HAYAAM: Wes ...
>
> WES: Yes?

HAYAAM: This morning ... there wasn't any blood.

WES: I know.

HAYAAM: Then we didn't ... ?

WES: No.

HAYAAM: Why didn't you ... ?

WES: If it happened, I wanted you to remember it.

They eat in silence for a moment.

HAYAAM: Thank you.

INT. HOTEL - LOBBY - DAY

Wes and Hayaam come out of the restaurant into the lobby.

WES: I'll check out.

HAYAAM: Not yet. I want to show you something.

WES: What?

HAYAAM: It's a secret.

She takes his hand and leads him toward the elevators.

> WES: Where are we going?
>
> HAYAAM: To the room for a minute.

INT. HOTEL - HALLWAY - DAY

They come down the hallway to their room.

> HAYAAM: Let me in. Then you wait here for five minutes. Then you can come in.
>
> WES: Hayaam ... ?
>
> HAYAAM: Please. This is very important to me. You will do this?
>
> WES: Okay.

Hayaam giggles like a school girl, almost blushing, and hurries into the room.

INT. HOTEL - ROOM - DAY

Hayaam closes the door behind her.

She walks to the mirror and looks at herself. She takes a deep breath.

She removes the bright hijab.

INT. HOTEL - HALLWAY - DAY

Wes waits. He looks at his watch.

He knocks on the door.

>HAYAAM: *(O.S.)* Come in!

INT. HOTEL - ROOM - DAY

Wes enters. His expression changes dramatically. He is shocked by what he sees.

>HAYAAM: Please close the door.

He does.

Hayaam stands across the room, completely naked.

>HAYAAM: No man has ever seen me naked before. You are the first.

>WES: Hayaam, I ...

>HAYAAM: Do you think I am beautiful?

>WES: More than I can find words to say ...

>HAYAAM: Good. Now you can go, so I can dress. I'll meet you in the lobby.

>WES: Hayaam, I ... right, I'll meet you in the lobby ...

EXT. HOTEL - DAY

Wes and Hayaam come outside.

>HAYAAM: What time is it?

Wes looks at his watch.

> WES: Almost nine.
>
> HAYAAM: I have to get home. I still have to pack.
>
> WES: When's your plane leave?
>
> HAYAAM: Seven p.m.
>
> WES: I'll get a cab.

EXT. HAYAAM'S APARTMENT - DAY

A cab pulls up in front of the apartment.

INT. CAB - DAY

Wes and Hayaam are in the back seat.

> WES: I wish I could see you off at the airport.
>
> HAYAAM: Of course you can.
>
> WES: I thought your father and brother ...
>
> HAYAAM: I would like you to meet my father.
>
> WES: You're sure?
>
> HAYAAM: Yes.

She starts to get out. Wes stops her.

> WES: Thank you. I'll never forget last night and this morning.
>
> HAYAAM: Neither will I.

She kisses him. A quick goodbye kiss becomes something longer.

EXT. HAYAAM'S APARTMENT - DAY

Hayaam gets out.

The front door opens and Abdul stands in the doorway.

Wes looks out the back window of the cab as it pulls away.

> ABDUL-HAKEEM: You spent the night with him.
>
> HAYAAM: What if I did?

Abdul slaps her, hard. He grabs her arm and pulls her into the apartment.

INT. HAYAAM'S APARTMENT - DAY

Abdul pushes Hayaam into the living room. Her father stands waiting.

> ABDUL-HAKEEM: She spent the night with

her American boyfriend.

JAMAL: Is this true?

Hayaam doesn't respond. Abdul slaps her again. Hayaam falls to the floor.

JAMAL: Is it true?

HAYAAM: Yes!

Jamal moves over her. He glares at her. Then he spits on her.

JAMAL: *(to Abdul)* Cut her hair.

Abdul tries to pull Hayaam to her feet. She resists.

He starts dragging her across the floor, toward the bathroom. She screams in protest.

Jamal watches with great sadness.

EXT. PARK - DAY

Wes strolls through the park, lost in his thoughts.

EXT. NYC - FREEWAY - NIGHT (EVENING)

A cab is stalled in traffic. Blinking police and ambulance lights are in the distance.

INT. CAB - NIGHT (EVENING)

In the back seat sit Hayaam and Abdul. Jamal is in

the front seat beside the CABBIE.

Hayaam wears a black hijab instead of her usual bright colors. She also wears dark glasses.

> CABBIE: Nothing I can do, folks.

Abdul looks at his watch. Jamal turns and gives him a worried look.

EXT. HARDING HOME - NIGHT (EVENING)

Wes comes out and gets into a cab waiting in front of the house.

INT. CAB - NIGHT (EVENING)

Wes climbs in.

> WES: The airport.

INT. NYC - AIRPORT TERMINAL - NIGHT

Wes enters the crowded airport. He gets his bearings and heads out.

INT. AIRPORT TERMINAL - ANOTHER AREA - NIGHT

Hayaam, Abdul and Jamal walk briskly toward their passenger gate. They clearly are running late.

Abdul sees their gate.

> ABDUL-HAKEEM: There!

At this moment, they pass a Women's restroom and Hayaam suddenly darts inside.

> ABDUL-HAKEEM: Hayaam!

Abdul and Jamal exchange a worried look.

> ABDUL-HAKEEM: I'll wait for her and meet you at the gate.

Jamal hurries off. Abdul waits outside the restroom.

INT. AIRPORT TERMINAL - GATE - NIGHT

Jamal and Wes arrive at the passenger gate waiting area at the same time. They don't recognize one another.

Jamal gets in line to board.

Wes looks around for Hayaam.

INT. AIRPORT TERMINAL - WOMEN'S RESTROOM - NIGHT

Hayaam pulls out a long section of paper towel. She takes it into a booth, closing the door behind her.

She looks determined, a woman with a plan. She picks up a full roll of toilet paper and sets it on the top of the basin behind the toilet. She starts wrapping the roll in the paper towels.

INT. AIRPORT TERMINAL - OUTSIDE WOMEN'S RESTROOM - NIGHT

Abdul continues to wait for Hayaam to come out. He looks at his watch impatiently.

INT. AIRPORT TERMINAL - GATE - NIGHT

Wes wanders among the waiting passengers, getting impatient.

INT. AIRPORT TERMINAL - OUTSIDE WOMEN'S RESTROOM - NIGHT

Abdul looks at his watch again. He moves away toward the boarding gate.

Behind him, Hayaam comes out of the women's restroom. She holds the wrapped roll of toilet paper high above her head.

> HAYAAM: I have a bomb!

Abdul turns and sees her.

> HAYAAM: Keep away! I have a bomb!

A woman screams. People begin to scatter in panic. More screams.

Hayaam moves, looking around in panic, like a trapped wild animal, the "bomb" held high for everyone to see.

> HAYAAM: Don't come near me!

Abdul makes a decision: he runs off toward the boarding gate.

Hayaam begins to make her way back the way she came, toward the exit, looking around wildly.

People give her room, some running off, others screaming. The situation is quickly getting out of hand.

INT. AIRPORT TERMINAL - GATE - NIGHT

Abdul runs up to Jamal. He whispers to him.

> ABDUL-HAKEEM: We have to board without her.
>
> JAMAL: What's wrong?
>
> ABDUL-HAKEEM: I'll explain later.

Wes has noticed this. He looks back in the direction from which Abdul came. He sees a commotion there and heads toward it.

INT. AIRPORT TERMINAL - HAYAAM - NIGHT

Hayaam continues making a circular, panicked itinerary toward the exit. People scatter at her approach.

> HAYAAM: I have a bomb!

Wes approaches and sees her.

> WES: Hayaam!

> HAYAAM: Stay away!

A SECURITY GUARD arrives, his gun drawn. He takes aim.

> SECURITY GUARD: Set it down!

> WES: Hayaam!

A second security guard arrives, also with his gun drawn.

> SECURITY GUARD #2: Down! Now!

Hayaam sees the gun and panics. She lowers the "bomb," held high until now, and starts running off.

A security guard takes aim – and fires.

One gunshot, two, three, and Hayaam falls.

Wes runs to her. SECURITY GUARD #2 holds him off.

The first security guard reaches Hayaam and kneels at her side. She is dead.

He removes her sunglasses. One eye is black.

He removes her veil. She is bald, her head nicked with cuts and splotches of hair.

Wes is grief-stricken at the sight – and the reality.

EXT. NYC - "GROUND ZERO" - NIGHT

Wes watches the night activity at Ground Zero.

EXT. NYC - "GROUND ZERO" - DAY (SUNRISE)

Wes has fallen asleep on the ground near Ground Zero. He stirs, wakes.

He gets up and stretches.

EXT. NYC - "GROUND ZERO" - DAY

Wes sketches at Ground Zero.

> HAYAAM: *(V.O.)* Dear Wesley. I am writing this on the day I am leaving. I will give it to Areebah to deliver to you. I need to explain so you will understand what is going to happen, what I've decided to do.

INT. HAYAAM'S APARTMENT - HAYAAM'S ROOM - DAY (FLASHBACK)

Hayaam wears the black hijab. She is packing as Areebah watches.

Hayaam picks up "The Rubiyat." She reads the inscription from Wes. Tears well up in her eyes.

Then she carefully hides "The Rubiyat" under

clothing in her suitcase.

Hayaam and Areebah embrace. Hayaam breaks it.

She fetches an envelope and hands it to Areebah.

> HAYAAM: *(V.O.)* I cannot go back after all. My brother has changed. My father has changed. I understand now that my life has gone places not acceptable to my family, and I have to choose between them. I choose my life.

Abdul enters the room.

Hayaam and Areebah immediately embrace. Abdul pulls Hayaam away.

INT. HAYAAM'S APARTMENT - LIVING ROOM - DAY (FLASHBACK)

Abdul drags Hayaam into the living room, where Jamal is waiting. Many suitcases are on the floor.

Areebah enters the room, fighting back tears.

Jamal nods to Abdul.

Abdul pulls Hayaam toward the door.

INT. NYC - ART STUDIO - DAY

Wes is working on a new painting from his sketches at Ground Zero.

Full of dark colors, blacks and grays. Suggestive shapes of death and destruction.

> HAYAAM: *(V.O.)* They will try and force me to go with them, but I have a plan. I know it will keep me off the airplane but that is all I know. I will be arrested. If you are at the airport, you will see this happen. When you read this, I will be in jail.

Wes paints with focus and energy, working toward his vision.

> HAYAAM: *(V.O.)* I will understand if you don't want to visit me. I have caused your family enough trouble already. But if you did choose to visit me in jail, of course I would want to see you. I can never forget you, Wesley, no matter what happens now.

In a lower corner, under the dark shapes of destruction, he begins painting a new theme, less abstract than the rest, and what takes shape is ...

–the small figure of a woman in a brightly colored hijab,

–the figure of Hayaam, her back to us,

–overlooking the rising dark swirls and shapes of destruction like a misplaced flower,

–an oddity of brightness in the overwhelming dark presence of the canvas.

HAYAAM: *(V.O.)* I will tell you something I could never tell anyone else. I am sorry I drank too much champagne. Do you understand what I am saying? I am sorry the first man was not you. Maybe one day it will be you if this is not too much to hope for. I try not to think too far into the future but this is hard sometimes. For now I am here in jail when you read this. I am wondering if you would want to see me. It seems to be the only thing I wonder about.

Wes stops. The painting looks done.

But there's one more thing to add.

He adds his signature at the bottom.

And above it: "For Hayaam"

FADE OUT

www.ingramcontent.com/pod-product-compliance
Lightning Source LLC
Chambersburg PA
CBHW060105170426
43198CB00010B/770